Mythic Realms

*The Moral Imagination
in Literature and Film*

MYTHIC REALMS

*The Moral Imagination
in Literature and Film*

Bradley J. Birzer

Angelico Press

First published in the USA
by Angelico Press 2023
© Bradley J. Birzer 2023

For information, address:
Angelico Press
169 Monitor St.
Brooklyn, NY 11222
www.angelicopress.com

978-1-62138-908-8 (pbk)
978-1-62138-909-5 (cloth)

Cover design: Michael Schrauzer

CONTENTS

Dedicated to my lovely bride, 25 years later:
Dedra

Introduction

"Images are representations of mysteries, necessarily," Russell Kirk, horror author and founder of post-war conservatism, wrote, "for mere words are tools that break in the hand, and it has not pleased God that man should be saved by logic, abstract reason, alone." Indeed, for Kirk, the imagination serves as our highest faculty. "The image, I repeat, can raise us on high, as did Dante's high dream; also it can draw us down to the abyss. . . . It is imagery, rather than some narrowly deductive and inductive process, which gives us great poetry and scientific insights. . . . And it is true of great philosophy, before Plato and since him, that the enduring philosopher sees things in images initially."

To be sure, Kirk was following in a long line of profound western thinkers from Socrates and Plato to the Stoics, Cicero, St. Augustine, Edmund Burke, Irving Babbitt, T. S. Eliot, and C. S. Lewis.

One might also see in these thinkers the praise of the poet as a romantic and creative individual. In his 1928 book, *Poetic Diction*, Owen Barfield, one of the Inklings, proclaimed: civilization "must look more and more to art—to the individualized poet—as the very source and fountain-head of *all* meaning." Here, Barfield followed Plato's ideas of "divine madness," arguing that not only did imagination allow one to understand his sense data, but also men "do not *invent* those mysterious relations between separate external objects, and between objects and feelings, which it is the function of poetry to reveal." Instead, Barfield continued, "These relations exist independently, not indeed of Thought, but of any individual thinker." Further, men:

> have lost the power to see this one as one. Our sophistication, like Odin's, has cost us an eye; and now it is the language of poets, in so far as they create true metaphors, which must *restore* this unity conceptually, after it has been lost from perception. Thus, the "before-unapprehended" relationships of which Shelley spoke, are in a sense "forgotten" relationships. For though they were never

1

yet apprehended, they were at one time seen. And imagination can see them again.

Such Platonic views mesh well with orthodox Christianity, which baptized the Stoic concept of Logos in the opening to St. John's glorious Gospel: the true light is the light that lighteth up every man. Importantly, St. John does not lay claim to only those who come after the Incarnation, death, and resurrection of our Lord, but rather stresses that all men—past, present, and future—are enlightened by the Logos. As such, even Socrates, Plato, and Cicero might very well have been enlightened by the eternal. In his own reflections on the Psalms, especially Psalm 119, St. Augustine noted that the "a lamp is a creature, not a creator, and it is lit by participation in an immutable light."

The Catholic Church "has always used imagination as the normal means of transforming a notional assent into a real one," historian Christopher Dawson wrote to publisher Frank Sheed in 1946; "the imagination becomes a channel of the life of the spirit like the other powers of the soul." Imagination "is a creative spiritual force," Dawson claimed in 1931's *Christianity and the New Age*, "which has for its end nothing less than the re-creation of humanity. The Church is no sect or human organization, but a new creation—the seed of the new order which is ultimately destined to transform the world." Importantly, he wrote to Sheed, imagination "becomes a channel of the life of the spirit like the other powers of the soul." This creativity of the Spirit alone will save civilization before it succumbs to self-destruction.

All of this ties into western notions of beauty, as well. "Nothing evokes this remembrance"—of things eternal and everlasting—"more intensely than beauty; this is a specific characteristic of beauty," Josef Pieper claimed in his brilliant little book *"Divine Madness": Plato's Case Against Secular Humanism*. "In its power to lead toward a reality beyond the here and now, beyond immediate perception, it cannot be compared to anything in the world."

Yet, in the end, it all comes down not just to imagination—which might be an imagination for good or for ill—but specifically to the moral imagination. As Edmund Burke explained in 1790 in his *Reflections on the Revolution in France*:

Introduction

But now all is to be changed. All the pleasing illusions, which made power gentle, and obedience liberal, which harmonized the different shades of life, and which, by a bland assimilation, incorporated into politics the sentiments which beautify and soften private society, are to be dissolved by this new conquering empire of light and reason. All the decent drapery of life is to be rudely torn off. All the superadded ideas, furnished from the wardrobe of a moral imagination, which the heart owns, and the understanding ratifies, as necessary to cover the defects of our naked shivering nature, and to raise it to dignity in our own estimation, are to be exploded as a ridiculous, absurd, and antiquated fashion. On this scheme of things, a king is but a man; a queen is but a woman; a woman is but an animal; and an animal not of the highest order. All homage paid to the sex in general as such, and without distinct views, is to be regarded as romance and folly. Regicide, and parricide, and sacrilege, are but fictions of superstition, corrupting jurisprudence by destroying its simplicity. The murder of a king, or a queen, or a bishop, or a father, are only common homicide; and if the people are by any chance, or in any way gainers by it, a sort of homicide much the most pardonable, and into which we ought not to make too severe a scrutiny. On the scheme of this barbarous philosophy, which is the offspring of cold hearts and muddy understandings, and which is as void of solid wisdom, as it is destitute of all taste and elegance, laws are to be supported only by their own terrors, and by the concern which each individual may find in them from his own private speculations, or can spare to them from his own private interests.

Burke sums this up so beautifully that it needs no further comment.

Acknowledgments

This book, *Mythic Realms*, began as a series of essays, an intentional follow-up to 2019's *Beyond Tenebrae*. Most of the chapters were originally written as individual essays for *The Imaginative Conservative*, *The American Conservative*, *Modern Age*, *The Epoch Times*, *Acton*, and *National Review*, though some were also given as talks, such as "Who Were the Inklings?" for a Hillsdale College lecture series, January 2022, and "The Haunting of Piety Hill, Michigan" for the Midwestern History Association. I offer each my thanks for allowing me to reprint them here.

I would also like to thank Angelico's mighty publisher, John Riess, for his encouragement and direction.

Additionally I would like to thank Mark Kalthoff, Paul Moreno, Chris van Orman, Steve Smith, Ed Gutierrez, Ken Calvert, Matt Gaetano, Miles Smith, John Miller, Scot Bertram, Tom Woods, Jason Jewell, Gary Gregg, Kevin J. Anderson, Winston Elliott, Stephen Klugewicz, Bruce Smith, Dan Hugger, Father Ben Johnson, Jack Butler, Dan McCarthy, Jon Lauck, Kelley Vlahos, Steve Ealy, John Grove, Peter Mentzel, Matt Bell, Doug Jeffrey, Kevin Gutzman, Aeon Skoble, Tamzen Meyer, Craig Breaden, Joel Haskard, Gwen Thompson, Sydney Hunter, Shelby Tone, Father David Reamsnyder, Todd Birzer, and Kevin Birzer.

My internet clan has kept me sane: Dave Bandana, Erik Heter, Kevin McCormick, Carl Olson, and Tad Wert.

My mom, Rita Feist, appears several times in this book, especially toward the beginning. My debt to her is immense.

I also want to thank my immediate family—Dedra, Nathaniel, Gretchen, Maria Grace, Harry, John Augustine, Veronica Rose, and Cecilia Rose (RIP). They even watched the movies with me.

Others, I thank throughout my chapters.

BRADLEY J. BIRZER
Feast of St. Thomas Aquinas, 2023

Part I: Personal Reflections

Authors Who Shaped Me, 1979–1982

Ever since attending first grade—at Wiley Elementary School in Hutchinson, Kansas—I've loved to read. I read just about anything and everything: from American founding fathers to UFOs, Atlantis, and the occult; and I read just about every mystery ever written for kids.

It was between 1979, sixth grade, and 1982, ninth grade, that I began to read according to author, rather than according to subject. It was during those years that my adult tastes began, shaping my thoughts (such as they were) as well as my aspirations. During those years, when I wasn't busy with school or my lawn-mowing business, I spent my free time divided between two activities—exploring the environs in and around Hutchinson (from oil derricks to wheat fields to abandoned buildings) and reading everything under the sun.

The first great author who meant something to me was Ray Bradbury. Sometime in fifth grade, I picked up a copy of *The Illustrated Man* and *The October Country.* I kept each by my bedside, reading one or two stories a night. The mystery of each story spoke to me, but so did Bradbury's language. Even then I recognized that he wrote in ways superior to most other authors. I found myself enjoying his tales of dark imagination but immersing myself completely in his vocabulary and writing structure. Soon, I was reading everything I could find by Bradbury, but I was especially taken with *The Martian Chronicles* and *Fahrenheit 451.*

The second great, J.R.R. Tolkien, arrived in my life during the third week of September 1977. My oldest brother, Kevin, was turning 18, and my mother gave him a just-then published copy of *The Silmarillion.* Though I did not understand it all, I read that opening— the creation story—repeatedly over the next several years. To this day, I can't read Genesis 1 without Tolkien's imagery dominating my imagination. Two summers later, I devoured *The Hobbit* and *The Lord of the Rings.*

Throughout 1979 through 1980, I read just about every science-fiction and fantasy author available to me, but Bradbury and Tolkien had given me a taste of the best, and I found myself reading George Orwell's *Animal Farm* and *1984*. Having recently re-read *1984*, I found the novel shockingly sexual, something I missed back in junior high on my first reading. Then, it was the repression, the resistance, and the rats that most affected me.

From my first books, my mom had ably guided and encouraged my reading. From time to time, she would simply hand me books and tell me it was time for me to read them. Usually, these became profound moments in my life. I'll never forget the first few pages of *Mila 18* or *Exodus* or *Armageddon* by Leon Uris. As with Orwell, with Uris I began to identify more and more with the oppressed. Of course, in hindsight, I see I was doing that back to my very first readings of the children's biographies of the American patriots. I also began to see wide sweeps of history, cultures, and religions.

At the very end of seventh grade—in May 1981—I saw Ronald Reagan speak at the University of Notre Dame, and political awareness entered my life for the first time. It was an utterly profound moment for me, and I fell in love with our fortieth president. Having grown up in a Goldwater household, I was already primed, but it was that speech at Notre Dame that meant everything to me. One of the many political books lying around the house—Robert J. Ringer's *Restoring the American Dream*—caught my eye, and I came to cherish every word. As much as I would love to claim Tolkien and Bradbury as my primary inspirations to want to become an author, it was most certainly Ringer's book, his arguments, and his writing style that shaped all my authorial hopes! I was so into Ringer that I became a rather obnoxious junior-high evangelist for the free society. Believe me, my classmates already thought I was odd. My newfound love only gave them greater evidence.

From Ringer, I rather naturally migrated to the works of Milton Friedman. No, I didn't read his monetary history of the United States, but I read with relish *Capitalism and Freedom*, *Free to Choose*, and his numerous columns in *Newsweek*.

In the summer of 1982, in between eighth and ninth grades, I began to prepare for high school debate. Part of that preparation involved meeting the grand master of debate and economics, Greg Rehmke, who introduced me to the works of Henry Hazlitt.

Toward the end of that summer, I read (consumed and devoured would be more accurate descriptives) and analyzed every little detail of *Economics in One Lesson* and *The Conquest of Poverty*. Whatever one might think of *Economics in One Lesson* as an economic text (and I don't have the skills to judge it), it was an extraordinary lesson in basic logic. I had read and outlined it so many times that I had much of the book memorized in high school. Indeed, nothing shaped my own understanding of logic more than did Hazlitt and, not surprisingly, the Sherlock Holmes stories of Sir Arthur Conan Doyle. Yes, I loved those as well. The arguments I encountered in Hazlitt and Doyle gave me great confidence to express my views in high school classes as well as in college classes.

From biography to high fantasy to rigorous logic. If I can offer any advice regarding my own experiences, it is this: don't censor what your kids read, but do encourage them.

On Loving Libraries

My earliest memory of entering a library was sometime during my first few days at Wiley Elementary School. It was the fall of 1974, and I had just entered first grade. Our school library at that point was simply a trailer located on/in the school playground. Whatever the shoddy construction of the place, it was magical. The first book I ever checked out—recommended to me by the librarian—was a biography of Lewis and Clark. I can still see, smell, and feel that orange book in my hands. It opened a world of possibilities to me. After that, I checked out books on Benjamin Franklin and the American revolution. Not surprisingly, I suppose, I have been fascinated by Lewis, Clark, Franklin, and the rest of that era all of my life.

The real mecca of my childhood, though, was the Hutchinson Public Library. My mom allowed me to bike on my own to the public library, 2.4 miles from our home. As early as first grade, I had my own library card, and I began to explore the rather extensive children's section. Every once in a while, I even snuck over to the adult section, perusing the mystical shelves of science fiction and fantasy.

Throughout my years in grade school, the public library also sponsored a Bookmobile, and I would meet that on a regular basis. The librarian even anticipated my arrival by pulling out certain books she thought I would like. In every case, she was right. I especially remember her introducing me to the myths of Atlantis and of King Arthur as well as to the fiction of Arthur C. Clarke.

In fifth grade, I became obsessed with the notion of research and writing research papers. In fifth grade, I begged my teacher to allow me to write a paper on the Pacific theater in World War II; an analysis of the Panama Canal in sixth grade (jointly done with another student); and a history of NASA space launches in seventh grade. By eighth grade, I had become so immersed in fiction that I spent all of my free time writing stories about a Paladin named Vortirian. Vortirian existed in a world all his own. Granted, it was a very Tolkien-esque world, but that world occupied most of my time (I had also given up watching TV in 7th grade and didn't return to it until my senior year of college).

But, in ninth grade, I joined the debate team, and my love of research not only returned, but returned with such power that it has never left me.

In Kansas, for better or worse, residents get their driver's licenses at age 14, with the restriction that the driver (for two years) drive only to and from school, work, church, or the library. Well, I took full advantage of this, spending hours at the library. And, I do mean hours and hours of wonderfully endless reading and endless research. Not only did I love debate, but things at home were troubled, to be sure, and the library offered not just an escape from domestic violence but an escape into the intellectual world.

My favorite librarian was Ms. Canfield. I really liked her at the time (yes, I had quite the teenage crush on her), but I admire her even more in hindsight (minus the crush). She taught me the card catalogue, she taught me how to follow one source to another, and she taught me the value of current events in the extensive periodical section. And I now realize how not just how intelligent she was, but also how incredibly patient and kind. Every time I arrived at the library, she gave me a smile, but she also gave me excellent advice. I especially remember her showing me how to use the *Reader's Guide to Periodic Literature* and other reference guides. At the time (being extremely libertarian), I wanted to become an economist (Milton Friedman was my absolute hero), but I also became fascinated with library science.

Research is a form of depth as well, a struggle against the flatness of the current world. In research, we follow one interesting idea, one author, and one source to another. When we search for Atlantis, we discover myth and we discover Plato. When we search for the Panama Canal, we discover Teddy Roosevelt, American ingenuity as well as American imperialism. Far from the flatness of internet searches, we discover hidden depths and meanings and nuanced realities. We also, critically, discover personalities. For what place or what idea or what innovation really exists without a personality behind it?

Between 1982 and 1986, I not only debated (which was my life, frankly), but I also attended Hutchinson High School. At that school, I had the blessed fortune of meeting yet another great librarian, a brilliant and hilarious man by the unlikely name of George Story. While I never had a crush (!!!) on him as I did on Ms. Canfield, I thought the world of him. He served as an extraordinary resource and inspiration to me. He ran the Monty Python club, and he also was a serious libertarian. I discussed ideas with him at school, and he even invited me over to his front porch for continued discussions.

While I never had a chance to get to know the librarians at any personal level at Notre Dame (undergraduate) or at Indiana University (graduate school), I have become particularly fond of the librarians at Hillsdale College, especially the now retired Linda Moore—who has always seemed to me to be as wise as Moses. Unbelievably witty, Linda has shown me, yet again, the virtue of tenacity in research.

May God bless the librarians of the world. Unrecognized as such, they are the keepers and preservers of culture, sanctuary islands in the maelstrom of turbulent modernity.

On Loving Research

I love walking through rows and rows of books, breathing in the dust of years and wisdom. At some odd and truly mysterious level, I desire to become a part of all that. From book dust you came, man, and to book dust you will return.

Some people talk about the moment in which Jesus saved them. "Yes, that was February 17, 1988, my junior year of college. I had always gone to church, but it wasn't until that night that I really met Jesus. At that moment, I came to know Him personally, and He took up residence in my heart." While I'm quite sympathetic to such a view, I have never had one of those experiences. My own experience was particular and it was grand, to be sure, but there wasn't any single moment in which I accepted Jesus. It was more of an entire serious of moments beginning at baptism and working its way up through the present, even as I type this.

For me, though, my life gained its clearest equivalent purpose when I was in fifth grade. I fell head over heels with words and books in early grade school. I devoured (the best word) innumerable books and tried over and over to become one with the written word. I did not just want to know how one wrote, but how an actual book was constructed, from typesetting and layout to binding.

These loves intertwined with a third love, my longing to know the recent past. I especially wanted to understand Kansas life in the 1930s–1950s. My maternal grandfather had served Army Intelligence during World War II, and my mom had been born in 1936. I knew the stories they told, but I didn't quite understand the context.

In 5th grade, Mr. Kinney began to lecture on his experiences in the Korean War. Born in 1967, I grew up with more vets of World War II and Korea than I could count. They were everywhere in Hutchinson, Kansas, in the 1970s and 1980s—running the stores, holding the offices, and sweeping the floors. I especially loved Mr. McKinney, though. His interesting stories were matched only by his many kindnesses.

Though he made no such assignment, I begged Mr. Kinney to

allow me to write a full-blown research paper. My paper? A comparison of the European and Pacific theaters of World War II. Outrageous, of course. Mr. Kinney, though, I think, was more than a bit bemused, and he gave me permission. I ran with it. Going through the public library as well as our own books at home, I took the project very seriously. Granted, my final product was presumably ridiculous to the point of absurdity, but that didn't matter much to me. I loved every moment of the process—from the initial stages of utter bewilderment to the compilation of data to imagining and completing the final form of the paper. With that project, however bizarre, I knew what I loved, and I knew what I wanted to do with my life. In some way or shape or form, I wanted to be a full-time researcher. Naturally, I had no clue what that really meant or what kind of jobs might exist out there. Somehow, I became convinced that someone would want to hire a full-blown researcher.

As I look back now, I realize that I desired full immersion into something that I could make my own. Growing up in the days of free-range parenting, I spent my days on bike or foot, exploring the environs of Hutchinson. A Saturday or a summer day meant getting up early, having a few bowls of cereal for breakfast, and returning home in time for evening dinner. My mom never cared what I did during those hours of exploration as long as I didn't do anything criminal or dangerous.

Research, I see now, was a way for me to explore without limits of environment, without considerations for weather, and without borders. Additionally, my mind needed something that demanded lots and lots of attention. I suppose even at age 11, I had more than a bit of OCD as well as a perfectionist streak. Add in that domestic life was, more often than not, horrific on the home-front, I was eager to escape—whether to Carey Park or to the public library.

To this day, I have never lost my love of research. Indeed, I can define every year of my education after fourth grade by the one topic I focused on each year: from the Panama Canal to the Milton Friedman-inspired research into Hong Kong to the Israeli raid on Entebbe to the pursuit of Hobbits into Mordor to the decisions of a Miami Indian chief during the American Revolution. These things and so many more intrigued me endlessly.

On Loving Research

Two things especially impress me about research. First, each project provides an endless, complicated puzzle, a problem to be solved, but never fully and rarely permanently. Follow one path and end here; follow another and end there. The possibilities seem gloriously unending. Second, the researcher comes to know his subject in the way a musician knows his music or an artist understands her painting. Research is an art, demanding full immersion, both in the gathering stage and in the compiling stage.

And, though I'm very near the end of this essay, I've still not touched upon the grandest of all forms of research: archival research. If a library is a heaven, the archive is even more so. Whereas the library is public, the archive generally is intensely private. Books, of course, are usually written for all who want to read, to read. Archival papers, though, are generally meant only for a party of two or, perhaps, three or four.

One of the most exciting moments in my life occurred in Ann Arbor, Michigan, in 1994. As I was researching the papers of the British occupying army during the American Revolution, I found a stash of love letters written by John to Abigail Adams. The British had intercepted them during the war, and they never reached their intended home. Yet, here I was, centuries later, reading the intimate words of one of the greatest men in the world to one of the greatest women in the world. The letters were love letters, but of the highest intellectual and moral levels. I realized that Abigail was not merely John's wife, but his equal, his best friend, his helpmate, his advisor, and his moral comfort. It was the kind of revelation that can only come from touching something so intimate, touching something that is universally true but only particularly manifested.

Let's all breathe the good stuff.

On Loving Words

From the moment I read my first book, I knew I wanted to be a writer. I can still see, smell, and feel that book, though I'm not sure I know the exact title any longer. It was a part of a series of reddish-orange biographies of famous Americans, and I remember eagerly devouring book after book in that series, each one in the same style as the Lewis and Clark one. Ben Franklin, George Washington, Daniel Boone, Davy Crockett, Betsy Ross, and others followed.

It wasn't just the story of Lewis and Clark that thrilled me, though their story has stuck with me ever since. It was the very construction and art of the physical book itself that moved me, even at age six. There was something sacred holding that book, or any book, frankly. The cover had been created with woven cloth, and the texture still resides in my memory, safely and lovingly held there for nearly five decades.

I don't want to suggest that I knew I wanted to be an "author" or to make a career out of writing with that first Lewis and Clark book. I was simply too young in first grade to know what such a career even meant, and I was still rather blissfully a small child concerned with the most wonderful of small-childish things. By the end of September of first grade, though, I did know that I wanted to learn to write and to write as often and as broadly as possible. In many ways, my desire was as much to make a thing called a book as it was to tell a story. I'm not sure I separated one from the other at that age.

From those early biographies, I leapt into the fantastic, and I was soon reading everything I could regarding real-life heroes (often mythologized) as well as histories of ancient worlds (seemingly rather fantastic) and fantasy novels—by Madeline L'Engle, Ray Bradbury, and others.

Soon after reading that Lewis and Clark biography, though, I started reading—as with so many first graders throughout the English-speaking world—the works of Beverly Cleary. I found my first fantastic hero in the figure of Ralph the Mouse with the motorcycle. At the end of the fall of my first-grade year, just months after knowing I would somehow spend my life writing, I wrote a story about Ralph the Mouse meeting Santa Claus. My teacher thought well enough of it that I was asked to read the full thing to the sixth-grade class at Wiley. My older brother, Todd, was in that class, and I'm sure my reading embarrassed him to no end. To me, though, I had made it as a writer! Truly, it was a moment of immense satisfaction.

Outside of what was going on in my family, five things dominated my life as a grade schooler: reading; exploring every nook and cranny of my hometown (equally on bike and foot); spending time with my maternal grandparents and aunts; caring for our quarter horses; and hanging out with a few close friends.

Whatever horrors at home, I loved my mom dearly, and she, more than anyone, encouraged any and all reading—whether of books, newspapers, magazines, or comic books. Her genius (and she is truly brilliant) inspired me to think ecumenically and broadly about reading and writing. Few, if any, things were forbidden, and my mom only insisted that we talk if I read or encountered something troubling, whether intellectual or spiritually. We never lacked for reading material, and frequent and beloved trips to one of the many used and new bookstores in Hutchinson and Wichita—as well as frequent visits to the Hutchinson Public Library—kept us well stocked in reading material. Indeed, when it came to books, my house and my upbringing were full of endless delights and treasures. We had a massive family Bible; biographies of all kind of statesmen; hagiographies of the greatest Christian figures; histories of many aspects of the world; travel guides galore, often with stunning maps and graphics; atlases (a favorite in our house); the University of Chicago Great Books; the *World Book* encyclopedia; subscriptions to *Time, National Geographic, Newsweek,* and *U.S. News and World Report*; and a seemingly endless sea of novels, high- and lowbrow. We spent hours just reading together as a family (not to each other, but quietly to ourselves), and we spent just as many hours talking about what we had read, what we had understood, and what was next.

My mom had inherited her love of reading from her father, and he—my maternal grandfather, Wendelin E (no period after the E;

just E) Basgall—was the most dignified man I ever knew. He read constantly, staying current with all in the world, believing it the duty of every citizen to read, to absorb, and to think critically about this world and the next.

I must admit, when I read recently about some advice-giver on Netflix claiming that a home should have no more than thirty books, I was horrified. I suppose there are people who grow up with few books around them, and, frankly, I pity them. Not only is the art of making a book sacred, but, when done well, the words within those books are sacred as well. After all, Christ came as the Word, and words, when properly understood, reflect His eternal glory and dignity, even if confined to ink on a page.

There are aspects of my childhood that I would never wish on anyone, and, to this day, I wrestle with them. But one thing I know for certain... my mother populated our house with books, and those books taught me not only respect for art, truth, and beauty, but respect for those who wrote the words and those about whom the words were written.

I may not have a Netflix show, but I can assure you, you will raise better children and families if you litter, clutter, and decorate your home in words. It might not be the highest way to honor the Word, but it's not the lowest, either.

On Loving Definitions

I first came across Russell Kirk's belief that academics must serve as guardians of "the Word" in his groundbreaking but now sadly neglected book *Academic Freedom: An Essay in Definition* (1955): "The principal support to academic freedom, in the classical world, the medieval world, and the American educational tradition, has been the conviction, among scholars and teachers, that they are Bearers of the Word—dedicated men, whose first obligation is to Truth, and that a Truth derived from apprehension of an order more than natural or material." If we love the Word—that is, the eternal Logos—Kirk explained, almost a full decade prior to his formal conversation to Christianity, we must also love and protect words. We must understand their definitions, agree to what those definitions are, and debate our ideas for this world and the next based on the first principles of the respect for the words themselves. As God gave Adam the power to name things, we maintain that duty and that legacy. Yet, it is not for us to change the meaning of a word based on our will or our whim. Just as common law is rooted in eternal truth but expressed locally, so is language. It would prove not only morally reprehensible to change definitions for light and transient reasons of pride and convenience, but also destabilize even the best of societies, as its members would endlessly speak past one another. "For the professor is respected, and respects himself, because he is master of a high discipline and the teacher of a traditional and valuable body of knowledge; he is keeper of a people's wisdom; he is the servant of the Truth, and of the Truth only," the then-Stoic Kirk argued. To serve the propaganda wing of a corporation, a bureaucracy, or a community is akin to evil itself.

In some way—perhaps in some mysterious way—I always understood Kirk's argument, even as a young child. As I mentioned in a previous chapter, I grew up in a house and community wonderfully surrounded by a seemingly endless sea of books. Whether I was reading a child's biography of Benjamin Franklin, a fantasy story about a mouse and a motorcycle, an action novel about the Jewish resistance to the Nazis in Poland, or a history of the Soviet Union, I cherished the word, the words, and the truth of words. I cherished them in isolation, and I cherished them within strings of words, whether as prose or poetry.

Thanks to a brilliant mother, I always had at hand the World Book Encyclopedia, two or three hardback dictionaries, and several thesauruses. I loved words. I loved knowing what words meant. And I loved chasing words from one to another. My mother taught me early on that I should never just skip over a word I did not understand. I should figure it out, first from the context and second from the dictionary. She also taught me, wisely, that a thesaurus is a guide, not a Bible. And it was not just my mother. The Dominican nuns who taught at Holy Cross grade school in Hutchinson also stressed the same ideas. Though I did not know this at the time, I was being given a very solidly Thomistic foundation for comprehending the world.

When I arrived in high school—a public high school, not the Catholic one—I immediately joined the debate team. Nothing in my education gave me as much of a foundation for my adult life as did debate. If debate had ever caught on like football and baseball did, I would have dedicated my life to being a professional debater. Major League Debate. The Debate World Series. OK, just a little bit of fantasy there… But yes, I learned once again in debate the absolute necessity of employing the proper definition of a word. If I failed to understand my own vocabulary, the opposing team justly took me down. If the opposing team failed to understand its own vocabulary, I went for the jugular. After all, how can anyone debate an issue if they are not arguing from the same objective understanding of the terms employed?

Throughout history, of course, tyrants and demagogues have always manipulated language for their own self-interest and political advantage. Perhaps no tyrants in history did this with more skill than did the Caesars in maintaining the language, institutions, and symbols of the Roman Republic while establishing the iron-fisted rule of the executive. To be sure, others have done the same. The grand sociologist Robert Nisbet went so far as to describe the entire history of the political state as the history of euphemism. What is surprising today, then, is not that politicians and bureaucrats manipulate language, but rather that American and western societies as a whole have fallen for the propaganda so easily and readily. Even with blatant warnings from Ray Bradbury and George Orwell, we have still fallen hard. Critical words—such "love," "myth," and "imagination"—have become things they were never meant to become, inverted, converted, and ripped apart until almost unrecognizable from their original meanings. Lesser words—such as "gay," "faggot," and "dogma"—have taken on entirely new meanings as well.

The traditional virtues have fared even less well, often ignored and mocked, indicating a wretched lack of respect for all that truly matters in this world. Few talk about fortitude, but justice has become vengeance, faith has become fiction, prudence has become timidity, and temperance has become abstinence. One best-selling author in the twentieth century even attempted to claim that selfishness is the highest virtue, thus diabolically displacing love from its proper place.

For any of us who identify with conservatism, we must understand and accept that one of our highest priorities should be to *conserve* the traditional meanings of words. After all, if we love the Word, we must guard our words.

Part II: Literature & Moral Imagination

An American Greatness: Willa Cather's *O Pioneers!*

Every once in a while, slow and steady wins the race.

One of America's greatest literary regionalists, Nebraskan Willa Cather (1873–1947), has only slowly and gradually been gaining recognition as one of our country's greatest novelists over the past century. Her first novel, *Alexander's Bridge*, came out over a century ago in serialized format in *McClure's Magazine*. The following year, 1913, she published her first novel-as-novel, the stunning *O Pioneers!*, taking its title from a Walt Whitman poem. For nearly a century, though, writers such as Ernest Hemingway and F. Scott Fitzgerald have overshadowed this brilliant writer from the central Great Plains, and it did not help her that she was literarily a romantic and politically anti-Progressive, anti-war, and, by the 1930s, skeptical of the New Deal. As strong as her reputation had been in the teens and twenties—with unadulterated praise from such formidable critics as H. L. Mencken—it began to crumble at the hands of the "literary realists" in the 1930s. To them, she insipidly took the worst of life and praised the heroic. Though a Pulitzer Prize winner in 1923, she never recovered her reputation in her lifetime, and her best friend burned her final, uncompleted manuscript, *Hard Punishments*. Since then, her reputation has risen and fallen over the years, but, today, thankfully, it is mostly rising. The state of Nebraska (culturally and politically) has wisely promoted Cather's reputation as well.

Cather wrote *Alexander's Bridge* as the kind of novel she thought New York critics would like. She wrote *O Pioneers!* not only for family, friends, and neighbors but also, most critically, for herself. "I began to write a book entirely for myself; a story about some Scandinavians and Bohemians who had been neighbors of ours when I lived on a ranch in Nebraska, when I was eight or nine years old." She found the new project "absorbing"—far more so than when writing *Alexander's Bridge*—and she, to her own amazement, realized that with *O Pioneers!* "there was no arranging or 'inventing'; everything was spontaneous and took its own place, right or wrong." As the book was written for her own benefit, Cather ignored all the things that she assumed the critics would demand. She thus feared that no one would think much of the novel, with its "slow-moving story, without 'action,' without 'humor,' without a 'hero'; a story concerned entirely with heavy farming people, with cornfields and pasture lands and pig yards—set in Nebraska, of all places!"

Yet what Cather did was create an American Myth: the difficult—slow but steady—story of a pioneer, a Swedish woman, Alexandra (no relation to Alexander in her first novel, but absolutely connected to that half-god conqueror of the ancient world, known as "The Great"), who yearns to love the land and succeeds in doing so. After all, when Cather introduces us to the story, she introduces us to Hanover (Red Cloud), Nebraska, and it is doing everything in its power not to be blown across the prairie in a gust of winter fury. The town, it seems, felt the ferocity of the Plain's wind below as well as around it. But when Alexandra looks upon the local area known as the Great Divide, it succumbs to her will. It is worth quoting Cather, here, at length, in all of her myth-making glory.

> When the road began to climb the first long swells of the Divide, Alexandra hummed an old Swedish hymn, and Emil wondered why his sister looked so happy. Her face was so radiant that he felt shy about asking her. For the first time, perhaps, since that land emerged from the waters of geologic ages, a human face was set toward it with love and yearning. It seemed beautiful to her, rich and strong and glorious. Her eyes drank in the breadth of it, until her tears blinded her. Then the Genius of the Divide, the great, free spirit which breathes across it, must have bent lower than it ever bent to a human will before. The history of every country begins in the heart of a man or a woman.

It would be difficult, if not downright impossible, to find a passage in American literature that better captures the spirit of American individualism and the frontier, the spirit of romantic longing and of temperate embracing. Cather, to be sure, captures all of the essence of Americanness in this passage. Contrary to critics who see nothing but the erasure of Native Americans, Cather's point is about human love for the particular harsh Plains landscape, a love that is perhaps unique to farmers who understand every inch of a region's rises and drops.

An American Greatness: Willa Cather's *O Pioneers!*

The novel *O Pioneers!*, not surprisingly, follows the story of Alexandra Bergson and her neighbors, Bohemian, French, Norwegian, and Swedish. Though not Roman Catholic herself, Cather writes so lovingly of the Catholic Church and the Catholic immigrants to Nebraska that she—as Notre Dame philosopher Ralph McInerny once said—might as well have been a Catholic in all that she did. It is, after all, in the Catholic Church that Cather finds the will to defy death and sin, nihilism and shame.

In her own understanding of art, which she often made explicit, Cather claimed that the true poet is immune to the drives of the marketplace. "Religion and art spring from the same root and are close kin," she wrote, but "economics and art are strangers." Almost certainly, thinking about the Progressives and the New Dealers, Cather meant that economists are the materialists and utilitarians who view the world as nothing more than a set of choices based on costs and benefits. Regardless, the Nebraskan continued, the poetry of a poet is

> his individuality. And the themes of true poetry, of great poetry, will be the same until all the values of human life have changed and all the strongest emotional responses have become different— which can hardly occur until the physical body itself has fundamentally changed.

O Pioneers! turned out to be the first of Cather's several books on the frontier, and her next novels—especially *My Ántonia* and *Death Comes for the Archbishop*—are not only superior but, arguably, the greatest novels written in the American experience. Yes, Hemingway and Fitzgerald, step aside! Contrary to their wallowing nihilisms, Cather is always humane and gracious.

In her 1913 novel, Cather wrote: "A pioneer should have imagination, should be able to enjoy the idea of things more than the things themselves." Amen, Willa, amen. The same is as true of a writer as it is of a magazine as it is of a critic. And it's just as true today as it was in 1913.

Slow and steady…

Over the Century Mark: *My Ántonia*

When it comes to considering America's greatest writers, it would be foolish to ignore Willa Cather as a contender. Indeed, it is quite possible that her 1925 novel *Death Comes for the Archbishop* is *the* great American novel, rivaling anything that came before or since. To be sure, Cather was consistent. While not at the level of *Death Comes*, her 1913 *O Pioneers!*, her 1927 *The Professor's House*, and her 1931 *Shadows on the Rock* certainly come close. Of all her novels, though, the one that most rivals *Death Comes* is her 1918 novel *My Ántonia*. When the book first appeared, that nastiest and most difficult of critics, H. L. Mencken had nothing but praise for it and its author. She is, he wrote approvingly, "isolated in accomplishment" and "isolated from all current rages and enthusiasms." Devoid of heroes, plots, love affairs, and any pretense to change the world, *My Ántonia* sees the world through the eyes of an immigrant, a poor Bohemian who becomes one with the land she works. "But what Miss Cather tries to reveal is the true romance that lies even there—the grim tragedy at the hearth of all that dull, cow-like existence—the fineness that lies deeply buried." Cather succeeds at making real and critical what is often ignored or hidden. "Miss Cather's method inclines more to suggestion and indirection. Here a glimpse, there a turn of phrase, and suddenly the thing stands out, suddenly it is as real as real can be—and withal moving, arresting, beautiful with strange and charming beauty," he continued. And then, surprisingly, Mencken offered his highest praise: "I commend this book to your attention, and the author no less. There is no other American author of her sex, now in view, whose future promises so much."

A full century later, Mencken's review still holds true. In almost every way, Cather writes at a level beyond every other American author. One could not be blamed, if giving any of Cather's novels only a cursory read, in believing her writing style somewhat juvenile and superficial; such a reading, though, would be dead wrong. In her many writings on the meaning of art, Cather criticized anything that might be blatant, political, or over the top. True art, she believed, contained the entire author's view of life, but it did so by layering, not by berating. "Art, it seems to me, should simplify," she explained. "That, indeed, is very nearly the whole of the higher artistic process; finding what conventions of form and what detail one can do without and yet preserve the spirit of the whole." Thus, she argued, the partaker of the art fills in all of the details of what the artist has intentionally trimmed and cut, making the art belong as much to the artist as it does to the recipient. "Any first-rate novel or story must have in it the strength of a dozen fairly good stories that have been sacrificed to it."

In this Stoic effort, Cather understood that nothing should be produced without every aspect of it meeting the highest standards of excellence possible. This applies to that which is seen as well as that which is not. As Steve Jobs would explain nearly eight decades later, every created thing should be excellent, in every one of its aspects. He cited the example his father offered him. If a carpenter makes a stunning oak chest of draws but uses press board for its back—presuming that no one will ever see it—the entire piece of furniture is junk. Cather, it seems, understood this. Additionally, Cather argued in the same vein as T. S. Eliot that no real art is revolutionary. Rather, it is always at its best when it's evolutionary. The artist knows when to compromise only when she or he knows the rules and knows what needs to be broken for real artistic progress. At first, every artist "is wedded to old forms, old ideas, and his vision is blurred by the memory of the old delights he would like to recapture." The artist, though, can only break barriers when he knows exactly what those barriers are. The writer, in particular, can never actually write about the essence of hate or love. Instead, he can only write of the human person as understood or distilled by hate or love. All emotion and ideas can only be understood in relation to character and person. If his own ideology clouds his art, the artist, in good conscience and taste, should forsake art and work "in a laboratory or a bureau."

Like the Great Plains about which the author so gorgeously writes, little that the eye first observes is true. The grasses one sees on the plains are nearly six times longer than those that grow above ground, hiding—at least traditionally—deer, buffalo, elk, birds of all kinds, snakes, and bobcats. Equally important, far from flat—as many crossing I-70 lament—the plains roll and break, thus giving a false impression of depth and distance. On clear days, one can see for miles and miles, day or night, even when the latter is not illuminated by the all-pervasive heat lightning of summer. The Great Plains unveil treasure after treasure to those who explore. The same is true of Cather's novels.

Though named after a Bohemian immigrant, the novel *My Ántonia* is really about the radically diverse life—human and otherwise—on the Great Plains, as understood by an emigrant from Virginia, Jim Burden. In the opening scene, Burden and Cather meet on a train, discussing their lost friendships of youth, including their mutual friend, Ántonia Shimerda, from Black Hawk (Red Cloud), Nebraska. Burden is now a lawyer for a large railway concern in the East, but he fondly remembers growing up with his grandparents on their Nebraska homestead. From the moment he arrived there from Virginia, Ántonia, though a few years older, dominates his cultural outlook and development. From the beginning to the end of the novel, she is a sprite, an earth goddess, and a force of nature, something fully human and yet superhuman as well. Everything that Jim thinks and remembers of Ántonia is synonymous with his memories of childhood and the country in which he grew. Ever after life had taken its toll on Ántonia's physical appearance, Jim could not help but see her inner greatness.

> She lent herself to immemorial human attitudes which we recognize by instinct as universal and true. I had not been mistaken. She was a battered woman now, not a lovely girl; but she still had that something which fires the imagination, could still stop one's breath for a moment by a look or gesture that somehow revealed the meaning in common things. She had only to stand in the orchard, to put her hand on a little crab tree and look up at the apples, to make you feel the goodness of planting and tending and harvesting at last. All the strong things of her heart came out in her body, that had been so tireless in serving generous emotions.

Married, but without any children, and financially successful, Jim recognizes that Ántonia—with her patch of land, her dedicated husband, and her innumerable children—has embraced and understood life at its most profound level. Jim can only describe Ántonia's land and family in mythic terms. Her children are fauns, and Ántonia herself is a "rich mind of life, like the founders of early races."

Though married, Jim admits:

> Do you know, Ántonia, since I've been away, I think of you more often than of anyone else in this part of the world. I'd have liked to have you for a sweetheart, or a wife, or my mother or my sister—anything that a woman can be to a man. The idea of you is a part of my mind; you influence my likes and dislikes, all my tastes, hundreds of times when I don't realize it. You really are a part of me.

For years, critics categorized and dismissed Willa Cather as a mere regional writer, a Nebraskan and little more. To a great extent, this was true, as Cather often wrote about the American frontier, though she was equally adept at describing it in the Canadian hinterlands, on the Great American Plains, and in the American Southwest. In all her frontier novels, she focused on three vital themes: the fundamental necessity of personal virtue and sacrifice; the communal effort; and the unforgiving but sacramental elements of nature and, especially, the land itself. *My Ántonia* explores all three themes. Those who came first either broke the land or, simply, broke. Those who followed rarely exhibited the same spark of life.

Those girls had grown up in the first bitter-hard times and had gotten little schooling themselves. But the younger brothers and sisters, for whom they made such sacrifices and who have had "advantages," never seem to me, when I meet them now, half as interesting or as well educated. The older girls, who helped to break up the wild sod, learned so much from life, from poverty, from their mothers and grandmothers; they had all, like Ántonia, been early awakened and made observant by coming at a tender age from an old country to a new.

Those who attempted to make it on their own—what in the 1920s would be called "rugged individualism"—almost always failed and went mad. The subduing of nature took the entire community. Having migrated across the Atlantic, leaving everything once known, the immigrants often fared best. "This family solidarity was that the foreign farmers in our country were the first to become prosperous." Critically, those immigrant farmers brought with them the skills, manners, and attitudes of the old world, usually expertise in food, music, the arts, furniture, etc., setting them a cultured step above the native American emigrants. Typically, though, the native emigrants took the immigrants' poor use of English as a sign of unintelligence.

While every sentence, paragraph, and chapter in the novel exudes a beauty, truth, and goodness, no one does more so than the tragic figure of Mr. Shimerda, the father of Ántonia and the one who first spoke the title of the novel. A gifted artisan and musician, he left Bohemia only at the insistence of his wife. He was a man of much intellect and skill, and his Bohemian community had always sought his advice and wisdom. In Nebraska, though, not only was he a nothing, he was incapable of understanding the land or working it. He became less than nothing, a burden to his family. Upon arriving on the Great Plains, he entered a deep depression. Right before Christmas, he killed himself with a shotgun.

In some unfathomable way, Mr. Shimerda became the spirit of the land after his death. Because he had committed suicide, no cemetery would accept his body. The family buried him at what would be a crossroads. Jim, though Protestant, wonders about the fate of his soul. "I knew it was homesickness that had killed Mr. Shimerda, and I wondered whether his released spirit would not eventually find its way back to his own country," he considered. "I thought of how far it was to Chicago, and then to Virginia, to Baltimore—and then the great wintry ocean. No, he would not at once set out upon that long journey. Surely, his exhausted spirit, so tired of cold and crowding and the struggle with the ever-falling snow, was resting now in this quiet house." Cather's passage describing Shimerda's grave is one of the finest in all American literature, well worth quoting at length.

> Years afterward, when the open-grazing days were over, and the red grass had been ploughed under and under until it had almost disappeared from the prairie; when all the fields were under fence, and the roads no longer ran about like wild things, but followed the surveyed section-lines, Mr. Shimerda's grave was still there, with a sagging wire fence around it, and an unpainted wooden

cross. As grandfather had predicted, Mrs. Shimerda never saw the roads going over his head. The road from the north curved a little to the east just there, and the road from the west swung out a little to the south; so that the grave, with its tall red grass that was never mowed, was like a little island; and at twilight, under a new moon or the clear evening star, the dusty roads used to look like soft grey rivers flowing past it. I never came upon the place without emotion, and in all that country it was the spot most dear to me. I loved the dim superstition, the propitiatory intent, that had put the grave there; and still more I loved the spirit that could not carry out the sentence—the error from the surveyed lines, the clemency of the soft earth roads along which the home-coming wagons rattled after sunset. Never a tired driver passed the wooden cross, I am sure, without wishing well to the sleeper.

Few if any novels have so captured the spirit of the American character, in all its majesty and nobility. Though many critics loved Cather, and her novels sold very well, her conservative politics had soiled her reputation by the end of the 1930s, and she became, in literary circles, a non-person for many decades. Only in the 1960s and 1970s did her reputation again soar. Today, Nebraska has done mighty things to keep the memory and legacy of her greatest artist alive. If you're crossing by I-70 or I-80, do not hesitate to stop at Red Cloud, her hometown, and the setting of all her Great Plains novels. Celebrate the mind, art, and imagination of the most American of American authors.

En route, if so blessed, you might just feel the spirit of a Bohemian, out of place and yet fully in his right place.

The Pulps

In a critical moment in the plot of Stephen King's *IT*, the protagonist finds himself distraught over a grade his creative writing teacher has given him for what he considered a first-rate story.

> The story comes back from the instructor with an F slashed into the title page. Two words are scrawled beneath, in capital letters. PULP, screams one. CRAP, screams the other. Bill takes the fifteen-page sheaf of manuscript over to the woodstove and opens the door. He is within a bare inch of tossing it in when the absurdity of what he is doing strikes him. He sits down in his rocking chair, looks at a Grateful Dead poster, and starts to laugh. Pulp? Fine! Let it be pulp! The woods were full of it!

Let it be pulp!

In current American culture, the word "pulp" generally signifies something dirty, quick, cheap, and maybe even quasi-pornographic. The word that might appear in the American mind immediately after "pulp" is "shoddy."

My mom always called it "trash fiction." This wasn't necessarily a bad thing. Some of the best fiction was trash fiction. It just wasn't "literary." *Peyton Place* might not be *The Republic*, but each could teach us something. I'll never forget when my mom handed me the former. She did it when I was the perfect age to understand it, and it taught me a lot about life, frankly.

The Pulp Era, in history, serves as a vital period in American literary culture during the interwar years of the twentieth century. There had been lots of pulp before the First World War, of course, but it became a major industry in New York and, to a lesser extent, Chicago, in the 1920s. Its growth rivals that of Hollywood, and each created the popular culture of the twentieth century. Not surprisingly, the two paralleled one another, and the predominate culture of the New York pulps, as in Hollywood, was Jewish and Catholic. Even during the years of the Great Depression, the pulps sold well, usually for a dime each. Out of the pulps came not only our comic book culture (movies, too), but the genres of science fiction, fantasy, and horror. The pulp culture also advanced mysteries and westerns, and as I sat in a darkened theater yesterday with my family, watching the latest *Star Wars* movie, I couldn't help but be reminded that *Star Wars* is rather—explicitly at times—an extremely modern and sophisticated take on the pulp serials of a century ago.

The pulp editors and magazines were out for profit, of course, but they also recognized that they had to distinguish their work in a vast sea of competition. Regarded by "serious" poets and writers of the time as pursing mammon, the pulps resulted in a number of artistic innovations, but, perhaps most importantly, they understood the basic elements of plot, the need to state a thing without softening it, and, most importantly, that the virtues mattered. At a time when Hemingway (whose style owes much to the best of the pulps, *Black Mask*) and Fitzgerald were questioning the very motivations of heroism, the pulps knew and proclaimed what was good and what was evil. Whatever his actual methods, the Shadow was nothing if not western civilization incarnate; his direct inspiration, Batman, even more so.

In his page-turning memoir of The Pulp Era, *The Pulp Jungle* (1967), Frank Gruber recounted how he had hoped to advance beyond the pulps into a higher realm of writing and artistic acceptance, the "slicks," his name for glossy magazines. Despite paying better, the slicks held no attraction for him once he'd succeeded in publishing with them. "The slicks did not satisfy me. I read the magazines and did not like the stories. Most of them were terribly effeminate, it seemed to me, and I was more at home with the virile, masculine type of story" (150). At the height of their popularity, around 1934, roughly 150 pulps competed with one another, the pulp gold standard being *Black Mask*. Trying to break into the market in the early 1930s and finding more rejection than not, Gruber remembered his vast output. "From August, 1932, through June, 1934, I wrote a grand total of one hundred seventy-four 'pieces.' The total wordage amounted to six hundred twenty thousand words, the equivalent of about eight books" (13). He submitted pieces to mystery pulps, romance pubs, sports pulps, and Sunday School papers. His postage bills, not surprisingly, were enormous, but he plugged away. Rejection didn't mean trashing a story, it just meant sending it to a new and untried publication the day it returned.

Though he often spent time with the rather Bohemian and dirty poets of Greenwich Village, they tolerated him only as a worshiper of the dollar.

> The Poets tolerated Steve Fisher and me. They criticized us freely and openly, calling us (at the least) commercial writers. Other times they sneered that we were selling our souls to Mammon. Well, I guess were trying to sell our souls, but Mammon wasn't buying. (61)

With incalculable will, Gruber succeeded. In 1934, he earned only $400. The following year, he brought in $10,000. From that point forward, with only a misstep here or there, Gruber wrote like a madman, for almost every genre and subgenre of the pulps—though he disliked what was, prior to the 1950s, called pseudoscience-fiction—and under a variety of pen names.

A number of great names, many of them essential to the maintenance of traditional virtues and western mores in American culture, emerged out of The Pulp Era: Lester Dent, Norvell Page, John Nanovic, Mort Weisinger, Julius Swartz, Max Brand, and Walter Gibson. As Gruber remembers, there really never existed a "Red Decade" for the pulp writers, unlike for Hollywood writers. Those writing for pulps in New York simply worked too hard to be political. And their readership wanted real heroes, not politicos, theorists, and revolutionaries. The vast American reading audience of the period wanted their men to be men, and their women to be women. They wanted legend and myth. They wanted success and failure. And, most importantly, they wanted good to be good and evil to be evil.

This also almost certainly explains why The Pulp Era remains the least studied period of American literature and culture. Our loss.

The Dark Virtues of Robert E. Howard

Dark Virtue

Shortly before his own death, pulp writer and somewhat maddened genius Robert E. Howard, aged 30, paraphrased some lines from Viola Garvin's "House of Caesar" and typed on his typewriter:

> All fled—all done, so lift me on the pyre—
> The Feast is over and the lamps expire.

On the following Thursday morning, June 11, 1936, Howard asked the hospice nurse about the health of his mother, who had, only days earlier, fallen into a coma. He had been sitting vigilantly with her for nearly three weeks as her health—never good—had declined precipitously. She had no chance to recover from the coma, the nurse informed him. She would never regain consciousness, and she would never again recognize him. Less than ten minutes after hearing the diagnosis, Howard had walked out to his car, taken a revolver from the passenger compartment, rolled up the car windows, and shot himself in the head. The bullet entered above his temple and exited behind and slightly above his left ear. Howard lived for eight hours before finally succumbing to the self-inflicted wound. His mother, Hester, died thirty some hours later, never having regained consciousness.

Howard's father, Dr. I. M. Howard, a local physician, had been carefully monitoring his son's behavior, as he had been very open about wanting to commit suicide should something happen to his mother. He especially did not want to witness her death. "I was watching Robert as this was premeditated and I knew it but I did not think that he would kill himself before his mother went," his father reported. In talking with the nurse, Howard had avoided talking about either his father or the attending doctor. "Had I known" that he had talked with the nurse, his father admitted, "I might have prevented this, because I know now that he fully had made up his mind not to see his mother die." Though he had written hundreds if not thousands of deaths in his numerous pulp stories, Robert E.

Howard could not handle the death of a loved one, especially that of his beloved mother. As one of his pulp fiction friends explained, Howard stoically chose his own exit from this world. Perhaps, too, there existed in him "proto-Nietzschean views," wrestling for possession of his soul. In a letter to a dear friend, Howard revealed his own nihilism:

> I particularly like the point you made in that truth and necessity not always coinciding, some religion is necessary for the masses. I have always maintained this, myself. As for myself, neither realism nor materialism appeals to me greatly. That life is chaotic, unjust and apparently blinded without reason or direction anyone can see; if the universe leans either way it is toward evil rather than good, as regards life and humanity. That there is any eventual goal for the human race rather than extinction, I do not believe nor do I have any faith in the eventual Superman. Yet the trend of so many materialists to suppress all primitive emotions is against my every instinct. Civilization, no doubt, requires it, and peace of mind demands it, yet for myself I had rather be dead than to live in an emotionless world. The clear white lamp of science and the passionless pursuit of knowledge are not enough for me; I must live deeply and listen to the call of the common clay in me, if I am to live at all. Without emotion and instinct I would be a dead, stagnant thing. . . . Defeat waits for us all.

In his own letters, Howard had talked openly about his melancholic "Irish" moods. "The fact is, I wrote while in the grip of one of the black moods that occasionally—though fortunately rarely—descend on me," he apologized in a private letter.

> With one of these moods riding me, I can see neither good nor hope in anything, and my main sensation is a blind, brooding rage directed at anything that may cross my path—a perfectly impersonal feeling, of course. . . . These moods are hereditary, coming down the line of my purely Irish branch—the black haired, gray eyed branch, of which as far back as family history goes, both men and women have been subject to black fits of savage brooding, which has been, in some cases, coupled with outbursts of really dangerous fury, when crossed or thwarted.

He had also, at times, written quite openly about the topic of suicide. Not atypically, Howard had written to the editor of *Weird*

Tales, Farnsworth Wright,

> I'm merely one of a huge army, all of whom are bucking the line one way or another for meat in their bellies—which is the main basic principle and reason and eventual goal of Life. Every now and then one of us finds the going too hard and blows his brains out, but it's all in the game, I reckon.

Again, it should be noted, this language was not unusual from the pen and typewriter of Robert E. Howard, who seemed, more often than not, to revel in personal violence in his imagination, however much he might avoid it in real life. Even, or maybe especially, in memories of his childhood, extreme violence crept into his thoughts. "When I was a kid, I had a few overgrown bullies make me miserable," he confided to a friend. "If I were to meet one of them today and he made any kind of move, I'd crush his damn head between my fists the way I would a cantaloupe." He admitted as much with his fiction, too. "When my fictional characters can't slash and slog and litter the pages with one another's carcasses, I'm an utter flop as a tale-spinner."

And, thus, on June 11, 1936, ended the life of one of the most interesting and talented men ever to be born on Texas soil. To write that he had been prolific as a writer would be an understatement of the highest degree. The man lived and breathed hypergraphia. As his first chronicler, Glenn Lord, has calculated:

> Between July 1925 and August 1939 (three years after Howard's death), *Weird Tales—Oriental Stories—Magic Carpet* group published sixty-four Howard stories. Of these, seven were serials. These required a total of twenty-one issues for their presentation. To put it in other words, Howard appeared in seventy-eight issues of that group, with a number of the chisel-reprints (no pay to the author) not included in the reckoning. In addition, he sold westerns, adventures, prize fight and other non-fantasy fiction.

He had begun writing professionally at age 18, and he had written continuously until his death at age 30. As just noted, he wrote for numerous and varied categories of pulp, and while some are rushed and somewhat artistically barren, many carried with them aspects of true literary genius, in terms of style and, especially, atmosphere. Yet this might have been a catch-22 for Howard, a reason for his own suicide. "I'm burned out. You pound out yarn after yarn—sometimes 10 or 12,000 words a day," he told a friend. "You work your damn guts out. Finally, you know you're burning out—that the time is coming fast when there won't be anything left. Nothing at all."

Best known of all Howard's works had been the wild and barbaric tales of Conan the Cimmerian, a rogue, swashbuckler, pathfinder, mercenary, and king, set some fifteen-thousand years ago in a mythic past, just on the edge of pre-history and history. "Conan simply grew up in my mind a few years ago when I was stopping in a little border town on the lower Rio Grande," Howard claimed. "I did not create him by any conscious process. He simply stalked full grown out of oblivion and set me at work recording the saga of his adventures." When two fans, P. Schuyler Miller and John D. Clark, wrote Howard in the latter part of 1935, sending to him an outline of Conan's history as well as their own map of Conan's world, Hyboria, Howard, moved by the outreach and dedication to his art, again claimed that he was merely the recorder and biographer of a Conan well out of his control.

> As for Conan's eventual fate—frankly I can't predict it. In writing these yarns I've always felt less as creating them than as if I were simply chronicling his adventures as he told them to me. That's why they skip about so much, without following a regular order. The average adventurer, telling tales of a wild life at random, seldom follows any ordered plan, but narrates episodes widely separated by space and years, as they occur to him.

Howard told his one-time girlfriend Novalyne Price Ellis that Conan represented some instinct found in every man, thus explaining the character's immense popularity.

> I wondered how Conan can be a real person, but I needed to remember that deep inside every man there was something of the barbarian, something that civilization could not destroy. A man reading this story about Conan, then, would feel again in the depth of his being those barbaric impulses; consequently, Conan acted as they felt they would act in similar circumstances.

Since his creation—or emergence, depending on one's point of view—in the early 1930s, Conan has become a staple of western popular culture, making his way into wildly successful novels (by Howard and others), role-playing games (such as *Dungeons and Dragons*), major motion pictures, video games, and comics. In terms of Sword and Sorcery—as understood by the vast public of pop culture consumption—Conan is second in popularity only to J.R.R. Tolkien's much more high-brow Middle-Earth mythology.

Critical Appraisal

Though there are relatively few academic articles, dissertations, and books on Robert E. Howard, his biographers have been plenty and never shy about the man's excellences. In the first full-length biography, *Dark Valley Destiny*, L. Sprague de Camp and Catherine Crook de Camp proclaim:

> With the instinctive insight of a great storyteller, Robert Howard seemed to know that Conan's adventures were a dream—every young man's dream of freedom, power, and unlimited success. He knew, too, that dreams should be amorphous, undefined, only hinted at, so that the dreamer may sketch in his own details. Because his readers are free to combine the artist's larger fantasy with their own less opulent fancies, Conan fans can readily turn Howard's dream into a heroic expression of their own hearts' desires. This, we believe, is the secret of Conan's immortality.

Several decades later, Mark Finn, in his excellent *Blood and Thunder*, wrote something comparable. There is an artist "who also blazed a trail in his industry by combining seemingly unrelated ideas to create something new, innovative, and completely unique. His name was Robert E. Howard, and he was the greatest pulp writer who ever lived." In 2021, Howard's latest biographer, Todd B. Vick, declared Howard to be "perhaps the greatest unknown author in the state of Texas, maybe even the world." Not surprisingly, then, Vick's *Renegades and Rogues: The Life and Legacy of Robert E. Howard* is a tour de force of the man's life and thought.

Some of Howard's contemporaries were no less fulsome in their praise. Most notably, horror master H.P. Lovecraft—a friend and correspondent of Howard's for years—believed Howard irreplaceable, his suicide a "worst knockout blow," for "his stories were the most consistently vital of all the voluminous pulp products."

Howard's "moody, neurotic side went deeper than we ever expected," Lovecraft lamented after learning of the man's suicide.

> Scarcely anybody else in the pulp field had quite the driving zest and spontaneity of R.E.H. He put himself into everything he wrote—even when he made outward concessions to pulp standards he had a wholly unique inner force and sincerity which broke through the surface and placed the stamp of his personality on the ultimate product.

Had he lived, Lovecraft claimed, Howard might very well have become "an important American regionalist" by making "his mark in serious literature with some folk epic of his beloved Southwest." Whatever the topic, though, all of Howard's fiction—even that written purely for profit—carried with it the vitality and genuineness of the man, as just noted, "and put the imprint of his personality on everything he wrote." His death at the age of 30 by his own hand was tragedy of the highest order, Lovecraft raged. "That such a genuine artist should perish while hundreds of insincere hacks continue to concoct spurious ghosts in vampires and spaceships and occult detectives is indeed a sorry piece of cosmic irony!" In the aftermath of Howard's suicide, Lovecraft continued, the forces of anti-modernism in literature had lost a grand ally and spokesman, and "fantasy fiction will not soon recover."

One of Lovecraft's admirers, Robert Bloch—who would one day write *Psycho*—despised Howard's writing. In a letter to *Weird Tales*, published in November 1934, he ranted:

> I am awfully tired of poor old Conan the Cluck, who for the past 15 issues has every month slain a new wizard, tackled a new monster, come to a violent and sudden end that was averted (incredibly enough!) in just the nick of time and won a new girlfriend, each of whose penchants for nudism won for her a place of honor, either on the cover or on the inner illustration. Such has been Conan's history, and from the realms of the Kushites to the lands of Quilenia, from the shores of the Shemites to the places of Dyme-Novell-Bolonia, I cry: "Enough of this brute and his iron-thewed sword thrusts—may he be sent to Valhalla to cut out paper dolls."

Not surprisingly, Howard's legion of fans rushed to defend his honor.

Not every modern critic has been so approving, either. In his masterful history of horror, *Danse Macabre*, best-selling author Stephen King has praised Howard for his ability to write horror stories—regarding his moody and atmospheric "Pigeons from Hell" as especially captivating—but has admitted that much of Howard's prose "was either unremarkable or just abysmal." Still, King labels Howard a "peculiar genius" who "overcame the limitations of his puerile material by the force and fury of his writing and by his imagination."

It should be noted that Howard might well have agreed with both Lovecraft (whom he admired dearly) and King. After all, he despised all attempts at literary modernism, the irony and sarcasm of an H.L. Mencken, and the loss of the heroic in modern literature. He was, he fully admitted, a wordsmith, a laboring man, little different (and perhaps less useful) than, say, a blacksmith.

> I admire the good artist just as much as I admire any good workmen; in fact, because of my interest in literature, I admire the artist's work more than I admire the work of other good workmen. But I try not to let my personal preference blind me to the merits of other good workmen. I have just as much reverence for the artist as for any honest and worthy person—and not an ounce more. I refuse to place art on a pedestal above and beyond everything else; I refuse to believe that a million generations of human beings have lived, suffered, toiled and died in order that certain men may make marks on paper or canvas.

True progress, Howard continued, came not from creation but from sacrifice. All real history, then, happened because some women and men were willing to sacrifice what talents and treasure they possessed for the common good of society and for the cause, especially, of justice. "As for me, I don't pretend to be an artist, or to love beauty particularly," he admitted to Lovecraft in personal correspondence. He especially wished he had more time to write poetry, despite his denial of pursuing beauty. "When you speak well of my work, I feel like maybe I have got something, after all," Howard wrote; "I wish I could give more time to verse, but the necessity of making a living crowds out." Yet, Howard persisted, he wrote for profit, for the ability to make a living independently and to avoid being under the thumb of any man. "I would not write a master-piece—supposing I could—unless I had the chance of selling it," he revealed to Lovecraft.

> That is literally true, but is not to be taken as a belittling of those who do write masterpieces without expectations of monetary gain. Remember that, such as I am, I am a professional writer. The money I get from my stories constitutes my entire income. I certainly couldn't afford to put in time on a "masterpiece" I knew I wouldn't be able to turn into cash. Naturally, I write loads of junk that won't sell. But I write it with the intention of selling it if I can, at least.

Clearly, two sides warred in Howard's soul as he thought about his own contribution to the world.

> I wouldn't sacrifice the freedom I have found in the writing game in order to become wealthy—if such a thing were possible—but I would quickly sacrifice whatever artistic ambitions I ever had. (I speak relatively; as you know, I am no artist.) I've heard a lot of people say and write that money was not necessary to real happiness; but I've noticed those people were always such as had never known what it was to be hungry, cold or thirsty, or wear ragged clothes, or work in the blazing heat or the freezing rain and snow. I wouldn't give a damn to be a millionaire; but I would like to be financially independent, and if the course offered itself, I'd desert the writing game in a minute.

As Howard and Lovecraft editors S. T. Joshi, David E. Schultz, and Rusty Burke have argued so persuasively, Howard viewed his pulp output during the Great Depression as "a means to freedom," a way to navigate independently in a world awash in control and power.

Decadence and Culture

Given the outrageously vast amount of pulp fiction produced in the 1920s, 30s, and 40s—what pulp writer Frank Gruber rightly called the "Pulp Jungle"—one must wonder what allowed Robert E. Howard and his Conan stories, especially, to gain such staying power over the past nine decades. Was it, as Howard himself suggested, something latent in the human soul that desired a simpler, more barbaric approach to a highly civilized world? Is Conan a representation of primitive heroism against a staid modernity? "The people who read my stuff want to get away from this modern, complicated world with its hypocrisy, its cruelty, its dog-eat-dog life," Howard told Novalyne Price Ellis. "They want to go back to the origin of the human race. The civilization we live in is a hell of a lot more sinister than the time I write about. In those days, girl, men were men and women were women. They struggled to stay alive, but the struggle was worth it."

Ellis herself claimed that Howard, however dour about the prospects of civilization, was a deeply opinionated and complex but otherwise humble and compassionate man with simple tastes and simple desires, possessing a complex and romantic sensibility when it came to traditional values. "I would say that he believed, basically, in the goodness of the simple life, and the simple man, with his simple ideas: that he himself was a good man, intense in his beliefs and willing to stand up for his beliefs; and that in his writings he was trying to say something—even in a pulp magazine, he was trying to say that this simple life was the ideal way of life," she explained. "Civilization had its drawbacks, it had its hypocrisies. What we needed was that barbaric simplicity of life." Ellis noted that Howard was especially loyal to and encouraging of his friends, whom he cherished, if sometimes awkwardly and clumsily. When asked in an interview about the sexual decadence—including pansexuality and sado-masochism—hinted at so strongly in some of the Conan stories, Ellis reacted strongly in a moderately feminist way about Howard's primness in real life.

> Oh, nothing was further from Bob's attitude. In fact, it was a little bit ridiculous in the other way. The big man was there to protect, to see that nothing happened. Never, never, by word or deed, I'll tell you this with utmost honesty, never by word or deed did he suggest anything out of the way. He treated me with the same devotion that you would treat something fragile.

Clearly, Conan was a fantasy, in more ways than one. Still, Howard persisted, our society was decaying rapidly, growing ever corrupt, and open and perverse sexuality was one of the most important markers. "You see, girl," he told Price, "when the civilization begins to decay and die, the only thing men or women think about is the gratification of their body's desires. They become preoccupied with sex. It colors their thinking, their laws, their religion—every aspect of their lives." Indeed, Howard went so far as to claim that civilization breeds not only depravity, but also the demonic, in humanity.

As a child, as one might expect, Howard had been particularly sensitive to bullies and conformists of all stripes. Though he did his best to hide in books—going so far as to claim that he raided rural schoolhouses for their libraries—he witnessed the complexities and nastiness of the oil boom in west Texas. Uncannily, Howard could glean the ideas of several books at once, according to his friends, and he could read the cultural landscape with as much insight and intensity. As much as he loved his home state of Texas, he resented those who came into it and, as he thought, exploited its resources for power-hungry corporations in the East. He is worth quoting at length on the horrors of the oil boom, as he understood it.

> You're right about oil booms—they bring a lot of money into the country and take more out, as well as ruining the country for other purposes. This might offend men in the oil business, but it's the truth that I've seen more young people sent to the Devil through the debauch and effects of an oil boom than all the other reasons put together. I know; I was a kid in a boomtown myself. The average child of 10 or 12 who's lived through booms knows more vileness and peace deal sinfulness than a man of 30 should know—whether he—or she—practice what they know or not. Clamor and filth! That's an oil boom. When I was a kid I worked in the tailoring business just as one terrific boom was dwindling out, and harlots used to give me dresses to be cleaned—sometimes they'd be in a mess from the wearer having been drunk and in the gutter. Beautiful silk and lace, delicate of texture and workmanship, but disgustingly soiled—such dresses always symbolized boom days and nights, to me—shimmering, tantalizing, alluring things, bright as dreams, but stained with nameless filth.

Whether or not Howard understood the whole picture of the boom, he clearly came to understand its seedier side. Overall, Howard feared, corporations were remaking all of America into "one uniform pattern, modeled on the mechanized fabric of New York," destroying the distinctiveness of localities, families, ethnic groups, and true communities and regionalisms.

America, Howard argued, was simply too big and, consequently, ungovernable. Had she been wise from her beginnings, she would have divided into several allied republics rather than become one big collective nation. Naturally, America should have divided into at least four geographical sections: the North, the South, the Northwest, and the Southwest. America, he believed, had only held together as long as it had because of the lingering pioneer spirit of the frontier, especially that between, roughly, "1795 and 1895," the high point of American liberty and felicity. All of modern America strove, however, to crush this frontier spirit of radical individualism.

> States' rights seem to be fast fading into nonexistence. Laws have become props to uphold big criminals and heels to grind down petty violators. Most of the present contempt for law seems to be the result of corrupt law enforcers—graft, fraud and injustice run rampant. A bigshot can get away with anything while ordinary men are ruthlessly trodden into the mire. There was more justice in the old days when each man packed his law on his hip. Men—at least in the West—recognize the rights of the individual, which are now ignored. Nowadays a man isn't supposed to have any heart, guts, brains, blood or honor. He supposed to crawl on his belly and lick dirt before the fetish of that vast, vague and uncertain idol Society—while the big ruthless ones trample that same idol with perfect impunity. I say Society is founded on the individuals who have individual rights. This was once recognized. An uncle of mine, a gambler who was well-known in the Southwest in the 80s, when on the witness stand, knocked down a domineering prosecuting attorney who was attempting to badger him. The judge only mildly reproved him, recognizing the fact that a man has individual honor apart from his obligations to "the mass" and a right to resent insults, on any and all occasions.

Soon, Howard cautioned, the only individual who mattered would be the extremely wealthy one who monopolized resources for his own benefit and self-aggrandizement. Once he had gained control of resources, he would pass laws (or have laws passed) that guarantee his own special privileges. "Once men sang the praises of the ephemeral gods carved out of ivory and wood," Howard claimed.

"Now they sing equally senseless praises to equally ephemeral and vain gods of Science and Commerce and Progress. Hell." Of course, Howard noted, the world—especially the European world—was even worse, with its various fascisms and communisms. "Europe, to me, is nothing but a rat den where teaming, crowded rodents, jammed together in an unendurable mass, squeal and gnash and murder each other," he wrote.

At home, Howard lamented, governments will soon turn to "massacre and wholesale slaughter." Such incidents were only a matter of time. Laws—too many to count—had come only to serve the wealthy. After all, he concluded, "we got more laws and taxes than we ever had before, and infinitely more crime."

> It looks like the courts, the laws, the government, all wealth and authority and power are combined to crush the last vestige of freedom out of the common people. Men that rise to leave the people sell them out and betray them. Where can a man turn? I wish I had vision, or a fanatical faith in something or somebody that creates an illusion of vision. All roads look blind to me. I see nothing but ruin, chaos, and a rising tide of slavery.

Being a good Texan, Howard remembered fondly when feuds, duels, and violence were private and freely chosen rather than enforced as policies of conformity. In America, though, no one in power would actually label any ruling policies fascist or communist, "but under the surface it will be the same old tyranny, modified, no doubt, to fit modern conditions." They could, he felt, employ "10 million high sounding names used to dress the real reality of slavery" while emasculating the entirety of the population. If the people ever realize they're slaves and rise up, he continued, they would merely start the whole bloody cycle over again.

Nihilism

As mentioned previously in this chapter, Robert E. Howard possessed a strong streak of nihilism, or what his friends called his "proto-Nietzscheanism." When Lovecraft confronted him about his view of humanity, he replied misanthropically, "To my mind the human race is merely a parasitic freak of two-legged fungi that pollutes the universe, which would be better off—and much cleaner—

without it. I have a strong prejudice in favor of life, but from a philosophic standpoint, honestly believe the universe would be better off without human varmints of any kind." History, then, had no real meaning for Howard.

> Regarding the various interests and time cycles and individuals— to me history seems mostly a chaotic jumble, through which move certain fairly well-defined streams and currents, but which is mainly too tangled for my comprehension. As I have said, I lack your universal and cosmic scope and comprehension. From contemplation of history as a whole, my mind retires bewildered and baffled and fixes on various figures which rise here and there momentarily above the general drift. It is the individual mainly which draws me—the struggling, blundering, passionate insect vainly striving against the river of Life and seeking to divert the channel of events to suit himself—breaking his fangs on the iron collar of Fate and sinking in the final defeat with the froth of a curse on his lips.

Human actions and free will meant little, if anything. "I believe that all human desires, aims, and pretensions are ultimately futile and empty, leading from nothing to nothing," with morality serving as nothing more than an ethical construction. In the grand scheme of things, Howard offered, man is no better than an insect, and a "baboon is as significant as an artist." On the matter of God, Howard declared himself an agnostic, but he had once been a faithful member of his local Baptist church. Religion, he believed, kept the masses in check, serving as a counterbalance to their more passionate instincts.

And yet, Howard was not always so nihilistic. For example, he proclaimed frequently his love of his family, of his Irish ethnicity (real and imagined), of Texas, of America, of the Southwest, and, especially, of his ancestors. He went so far as to argue that he had either lived previous lives or that he carried with him all the memories of his ancestors. "I've lived before. I remember it," he told Price. "My ancestors came from a cold, bleak island, and I feel their blood beating in my veins." To Lovecraft, he explained at some length:

> I believe that many dreams are the result of ancestral memories, handed down through the ages. I have lived in the Southwest all

my life yet most of my dreams are laid in cold, giant lands of icy wastes in gloomy skies, and of wild, windswept fens and wildernesses over which sweep great sea winds, and which are inhabited by shock-headed savages with light fierce eyes. With the exception of that one dream I described to you, I am never, in these dreams of ancient times, a civilized man. Always I am the barbarian, the skin-clad, tousle-haired, wide-eyed wild man, armed with a rude axe or sword, fighting the elements and wild beasts, or grappling with armored hosts marching with the tread of civilized discipline, from fellow fruitful lands and walled cities. This is reflected in my writings, too, for when I began a tale of old times, I always find myself instinctively arrayed on the side of the barbarian, against the powers of organized civilization.

Conclusion

Questions cloud the memory of Robert E. Howard. Why, for example, Howard committed suicide has remained a mystery—a rather perplexing one—for his fans for nearly a century now. Perhaps he could not imagine his mother dying. Perhaps he had run out of things to write. Perhaps his mother was his lifeline to navigate against modernity. Perhaps, in some Stoic fashion, he simply wanted to take command of his own life. Perhaps his nihilism had finally gotten the best of him. Or, perhaps, he was mentally unbalanced or ill. Each of these reasons—or at least some part and combination of each of them—seems plausible, but none truly satisfy.

Equally important, one might legitimately wonder what Howard would have written and what path his writing career would have taken. Toward the end of his life, when not lamenting a dryness in his productivity, Howard expressed much interest in writing two things. First, he wanted to continue to write as many pulp westerns—of which he wrote both tall tales and weird tales—and to write either a history or a historical novel set in the American Southwest. Not surprisingly, Howard was quite good on western subjects, and his westerns—tall or weird—possess a higher literary standard than did his fantasy stories. They feel, for lack of a better term, less pulpish. Given the changes in the entertainment industry, there is no reason to presume that Howard might not have written his own *Stagecoach* or *Shane*, or perhaps, in the 1950s and 1960s, written for any one of a number of television programs. He had, after all, the speed and the imagination.

Yet, these things must remain "what ifs." The fact of the matter is, Robert E. Howard's life and career ended on June 11, 1936, by his own hand and of his own free will. Still, in just thirty short years, he carved out his own path, lived according to his own definition of freedom, espoused some dark virtues in his fiction, and navigated the insanities of modernity rather beautifully.

Too bad it had to end so tragically.

C. S. Lewis and the Truth of Balder

As is well known, C.S. Lewis converted to Christianity in the fall of 1931 after a long, late-night discussion with Hugo Dyson and J.R.R. Tolkien on September 13, 1931. As he beautifully described the evening in a letter to a close friend, Lewis wrote: "We began (in Addison's walk just after dinner) on metaphor and myth—interrupted by a rush of wind which came so suddenly on the still, warm evening and sent so many leaves pattering down that we thought it was raining." One must wonder if it could have been more inspirational or romantic. Yes, it turns out, it could. "We all held our breath, the other two appreciating the ecstasy of such a thing." A full month later, the determined Lewis offered a few more details to his correspondent. What he learned from Dyson and Tolkien that night, he wrote in a personal letter, was that

> if I met the idea of sacrifice in a Pagan story I didn't mind it at all: again, that if I met the idea of a god sacrificing himself to himself. . . . I liked it very much and was mysteriously moved by it: again, that the idea of the dying and reviving god (Balder, Adonis, Bacchus) similarly moved me provided I met it anywhere except in the Gospels.

The mythic versions, he admitted, gave him a certain distance that allowed him, ironically, to embrace the very essence of the story, if finding the accidents of the stories unbelievable. The conversation with Dyson and Tolkien, though, allowed Lewis, for the first time in his life, to see that Christianity expresses not just myth, but true myth, something profoundly real, "a myth working on us in the same way as the others, but with this tremendous difference that it really happened."

Understandably, given Lewis's status as the greatest Christian apologist of the twentieth century, this explanation has perplexed Christians for over half a century. Is Christianity myth or truth? Is it fact or not?

To understand this, one must take into account the myth that moved Lewis. Even though he mentioned three gods in his 1931 letter, he really cared most about Balder. "I had become fond of Long-fellow's Saga of King Olaf: fond of it in a casual, shallow way for its story and its vigorous rhythms," Lewis recorded in his autobiography, *Surprised by Joy.*

> But then, and quite different from such pleasures, and like a voice from far more distant regions, there came a moment when I idly turned the pages of the book and found the unrhymed translation of *Tegner's Drapa* and read: "I heard a voice that cried, 'Balder the beautiful is dead, is dead.'"

The words seemed to have come from infinity itself, and Lewis had no context for them, knowing them only, somehow, to express truth. "I knew nothing about Balder; but instantly I was uplifted into huge regions of northern sky, I desired with almost sickening intensity something never to be described (except that it is cold, spacious, severe, pale, and remote) and then, as in the other examples, found myself at the very same moment already falling out of that desire and wishing I were back in it."

The story of Balder is one of the oldest in the Northern tradition, and it makes its way into a number of different Scandinavian myths and sagas. Always referred to as Balder (Baldr, Baldar) the Beautiful or the Good and a son of Odin, he experienced terrible nightmares that suggested some imminent danger. Worried, Odin descended into Hell and raised the corpse of a dead witch, seeking her advice and knowledge. Trying to hide his identity from her, Odin forces her to speak, though she is beyond reluctant to do so. Finally exhausting herself beyond recovery, she names Odin as the desecrator of her death. Upset that she has discovered his identify, he curses her. "You are not a prophetess nor a wise woman," he yells. "Rather you are the mother of three ogres." Mockingly, she retorts: "Ride home, Odin, and be proud of yourself! No more men will come to visit me, until Loki is loose, escaped from his bonds, and the Doom of the Gods, tearing all asunder, approaches."

When Balder explained his dreams to the other gods, they decided to weave as many spells of protection about him as possible, but they did this mostly by demanding an oath from all created things that they would not harm Balder. Becoming seemingly invincible, the gods amused themselves by attacking Balder, knowing him to be invulnerable. In the west of Valhalla, though, grew one tiny plant that the gods had neglected to tame, mistletoe. Learning of this, the trickster of tricksters, Loki, broke a stick from the mistletoe, giving it to the blind god, Hod. He then encouraged Hod to participate in the "hit Balder" games by attacking with the stick. Unwittingly, Hod killed Balder. Shocked beyond understanding, the gods realized they were mortal. They lost all confidence in themselves and desired to slay Loki for his fell deeds. Honoring Balder, the gods placed him upon the largest ship available, setting it afire. In grief, Balder's wife dropped dead, and even a dwarf found himself accidentally kicked into the fire by a distraught Thor.

One of Balder's brothers, Hermod, rode into Hell itself to find Balder. There, he discovered his brother sitting "in a seat of honor." As proof of his safety, Balder gave his brother a golden ring—Draupnir—to take to the world of the living and to Asgard, home of the gods. Hermod then sought all of the world to "weep for Balder," thus releasing him from the dead. All creatures wept except for Thokk, a giantess who felt she owed nothing to the gods. "Let Hel hold what she has," Thokk declared.

With the death of the gods during Ragnarök, the seeress had told Odin when he had forced her from the sleep of dead, Balder will return and help make the world—if only for a time—a paradise. Even this, though, will ultimately fail, as the flying serpent Nidhogg will descend and carry the dead in his wings.

Though unrelentingly pagan, Balder's story—and the stories of his fellow gods—parallels the stories of Saul and Jesus in scripture.

As Lewis so wisely argued in the weeks following his conversion to Christianity:

> The pagan stories are God expressing Himself through the minds of the poets, using such images as He found there, while Christianity is God expressing Himself through what we call "real things." Therefore it is true, not in the sense of being a "description" of God (that no finite mind could take in) but in the sense of being the way in which God chooses to (or can) appear to our faculties.

Balder is dead, to be sure. But Christ is quite alive.

Who Were the Inklings?[1]

"Tollers," C.S. Lewis declared, using one of the many names—nicked as well as given—of his good friend John Ronald Reuel Tolkien. "There is too little of what we really like in stories. I am afraid we shall have to try and write some ourselves."

Though Tolkien did not record the exact date of this conversation, it almost certainly happened sometime in the mid-1930s, probably 1936. Tolkien had already written but had not published *The Hobbit*, and he would soon write his most famous academic essays on Beowulf and "On Fairy-Stories." He also held a chair at the University of Oxford at Pembroke College, soon to be followed by the even more prestigious Merton Chair at Merton College. Lewis, however, held the much less prestigious position of Fellow at Magdalen College, Oxford, but his writing career was at nearly the same stage as Tolkien's. By the mid 1930s, he had written his first significant piece of scholarship, "A Note on Comus," as well as his excellent *Allegory of Love*, but after his conversion to Christianity in September and October of 1931, he had also begun to write Christian apologetics in a variety of forms. The first significant such book was his *Pilgrim's Regress*, after which his great friend Owen Barfield said Lewis "never looked back, but appeared to my dazzled eyes to go on for the rest of his life writing more and more successful books at shorter and shorter intervals."

Would it be possible, Tolkien and Lewis wondered in the 1930s, to write fiction that might combine all of these things: a love of history; a desire to debate the defenders of the modern world and point out the many foibles of modern living; and a way to promote one's philosophical and religious beliefs without being overly blatant? That is, could a modern writer create art while avoiding the pitfalls

1. This was a talk given on January 30, 2022, for Hillsdale's Center for Constructive Alternatives. I would like to thank the students of my Christian Humanism class (Spring 2022); Nathaniel and Dedra Birzer; Matt Bell, Doug Jeffrey, and Tim Caspar of the CCA office; and Dean Mark Kalthoff, Eric Hutchinson, Nathan Schlueter, and Jason Peters of the faculty roundtable.

of the ever-prevalent ideological morass and political propaganda of the era and remain artful?

After a "toss up," the two men agreed that Lewis's stories would deal with space travel while Tolkien's would deal with time travel. It should be remembered that the term "science fiction" did not yet exist in the 1930s—except among a few pockets of followers, here and there—and would not become the accepted term for that genre until the very early 1950s. While other writers such as Thomas More, Mark Twain, G. K. Chesterton, H. G. Wells, and Aldous Huxley had already produced what would be one day called and labeled science fiction, Tolkien and Lewis's decision to write of such things was quite out of the ordinary. So much so that the average person of the English-speaking world regarded what would be known as science-fiction as something at once conflictingly juvenile and porno-graphic, the stuff merely of pulp. What Tolkien and Lewis were really hoping to create, and succeeded in doing so, was myth and faerie. Lewis's books that came from this friendly competition— *Out of the Silent Planet*, *Perelandra*, and *That Hideous Strength*— became immediately successful and propelled him into the public eye in the U.K. and in North America and helped legitimize science fiction throughout the English-speaking world. Indeed, one could go so far as to state that C. S. Lewis and Ray Bradbury made science fiction respectable. Tolkien's attempt at a time-travel story failed in the short term, though, and it would take two more decades for *The Lord of the Rings* to appear and another two decades after that for *The Silmarillion* to be published. In the four decades since *The Silmarillion* first appeared, however, at least fifteen more volumes of Tolkien's imaginary world of Middle Earth have been edited and published by his son, the now late Christopher.

Additionally, it seems, the two decided to allow one another free rein to create what they would. Inspired by the fear that space travel would allow men to ignore sin and believe that technology could triumph over all in the universe, Lewis decided to write his story as a cautionary one against imperialism while also including rather traditional Christian theology and incorporating and baptizing pagan mythology. By the third of the trilogy, *That Hideous Strength*, however, Lewis had borrowed significantly from Tolkien's invented

Atlantean world of Númenor. Númenor, corrupted as "Numinor," appears nine times in *That Hideous Strength* as well as in one of Lewis's poems, "The End of the Wine," and, very likely, as the background to Atlantis in the Narnia tale *The Magician's Nephew*. Not surprisingly, especially given Tolkien's rather eccentric as well as individualistic character, he took nothing from Lewis except the inspiration to work hard and keep his fortitude as stoically as possible. Completely unrelated to anything Lewis wrote or created, Tolkien's own time-travel story became intimately a part of his larger mythology, incorporated as the touchstone of the Second Age of the World, a world in which men rose and fell.

In almost every way, this challenge fits the friendship as well as the personalities of Lewis and of Tolkien rather perfectly. Tolkien niggled, a perfectionist seeking nothing less than the true, the good, and the beautiful. Lewis, a bolt of lightning and a force of nature, never stopped, as though his mind and soul were incapable of true rest, hesitation, or relaxation. Whereas *That Hideous Strength* is one of the finest, if not *the* finest, dystopias of the twentieth century, it flawlessly captures the fears and the delusions of right-wing and left-wing progressivism of the 1940s. In grand contrast, *The Lord of the Rings*, published a decade later, reveals and explores the very essence of human existence. If *That Hideous Strength*, probably Lewis's greatest work (along with the *Abolition of Man*), was the Christian *1984* of its time, *The Lord of the Rings* is the greatest tale of modernity, comparable to Virgil's *The Aeneid*, the great tale of the ancient world, and Dante's *Divine Comedy*, the great tale of the medieval world. Indeed, while many might very well see this following as the throwing down of the gauntlet by an unrelenting patriot and partisan, it is not too radical to believe that five hundred years from now, the world will view *The Lord of the Rings* and its associated mythology in the way we of the 21st-century view Milton, Dante, Virgil, and Homer as representatives of their respective eras.

And yet whatever their differences in personality, in religious outlook, and in artistic achievement, Tolkien cannot be separated from Lewis, and Lewis cannot be separated from Tolkien. The two belong together as readily as Lewis and Clark, as surely as Holmes and Watson, as certainly as Chesterton and Belloc, and as wonderfully as Batman and Robin. Their friendship, quite real, was nothing less than one of the greatest friendships of its century. Where the two gathered, they coalesced, changed, and became something greater than they had been alone as individuals, no matter what level or type of genius each possessed. Through their friendship—and especially its most important manifestation, the Inklings—Tolkien and Lewis created what their mutual friend Owen Barfield would call in 1940 a "commonwealth of the spirit in which there is no copyright."

Yet, whatever love and admiration Tolkien and Lewis shared for one another, and despite the never-ending inspiration each gave to the other, the two often found themselves out of sync. Lewis, that force of nature, started things too quickly, borrowed from others too freely, and rarely cared what another thought of him. Tolkien, that gentleman of wisdom, moved slowly and observed everything, desired originality and depth to a fault, and worried constantly about what he said and what others said. Nothing is so revelatory of their personalities as the way Oxford thought of each and they of Oxford. Most students admired Tolkien and Lewis, but they adored Tolkien as a fatherly and a grandfatherly figure, while they feared (and admired) Lewis as a bulldog—odd, and sometimes rabid in his criticisms. Almost a fop, Tolkien appeared anywhere and everywhere with handsome dignity. A bachelor throughout most of his life, Lewis seemingly considered it unmanly and vain to care about one's appearance. He reeked of various types of tobacco, and his wardrobe clothed him rather shabbily. Among their equals and academic peers, however, Lewis possessed the thick skin of a dragon's hide, while Tolkien allowed every comment to become a slight, accumulating them as a type of "death by a thousand cuts."

And yet… what a friendship. Each loved myth, honesty, and God. Each desired to make the world a better place, and each knew the other as a vital ally in making such a thing happen. Most importantly, the two men loved one another, whatever specific troubles might have hung over them, real or imagined. Certainly, each thought the other a genius and a rarity in this world of sorrows, violence, and upheavals.

The two met for the first time at a faculty meeting on May 11,

1926. Lewis famously wrote in his autobiography, *Surprised by Joy*, that as a Protestant Ulsterman, he had been taught all of his life never to trust a papist, and, in his academic life, never to trust a philologist. Tolkien, Lewis notes rather humorously, was both! A year later, in 1927, Tolkien founded the Koalbiters, a group dedicated to learning Icelandic (that is, Old Norse) and reading the great sagas and eddas of the Northern Middle Ages, seeing these as a means to promote a very particular understanding of Anglo-Saxon language, history, and culture. On October 17, 1929, the two men became something more than academic colleagues who admired one another. For, on this day, Tolkien and Lewis admitted to one another that they had an almost childlike love of all things northern, mythologically, the "gods and giants and Asgard." They talked for three hours that night about such things. Even more importantly, this conversation led to Tolkien admitting that he had been working on his own mythological world—his Legendarium, he called it—for well over a decade. This had been little more than a private hobby with a few poetic manifestations up to this point in Tolkien's life, and only his closest friends and family knew anything of this. He even lent a copy of his "Lay of Leithian" to Lewis, following this meaningful conversation. Two months later, Lewis offered Tolkien the following response. "I sat up late last night and have read the Geste as far as to where Beren and his gnomish allies defeat the patrol of orcs above the sources of the Narog and disguise themselves in the reaf," an Anglo-Saxon term for clothing and weapons taken from the dead. "I can quite honestly say that it is ages since I have had an evening of such delight." As Lewis did for so many of his friends, he bolstered Tolkien's creative spirit and tenacity, challenging him to do better and perfect what already seemed nearly perfect.

Tolkien also continued to talk with Lewis about religion, myth, and, in particular, Christianity, trying to wean his friend of his quasi-atheistic views. On the evening of September 18 and into the early morning of September 19, 1931, Tolkien, another friend, Hugo Dyson, and Lewis talked about the relationship of pagan mythology to Christian theology. That conversation, more than anything else in his life, convinced Lewis to become a full-blown adherent of

Christianity. "We began," Lewis noted in a personal letter, "on metaphor and myth—interrupted by a rush of wind which came so suddenly on the still, warm evening and sent so many leaves pattering down that we thought it was raining. We all held our breath, the other two appreciating the ecstasy of such a thing." His convictions became so strongly evangelical from this moment until the end of his days that it almost completely pervaded and overwhelmed his already boisterous personality. In some way that probably only God understands, Lewis became not just Christian that night, but much more fully C. S. Lewis.

Two years after Lewis converted to Christianity, in the summer of 1933, the remnants of the group that had once been known as the Koalbiters had expanded (or mutated, depending on one's perspective) to include many of Lewis's closest friends and began to call itself "The Inklings." The group of friends would have come into existence no matter its name, Tolkien claimed, as Lewis had a profound love of all of the things the Inklings would come to do so well. Lewis, especially, "had a passion for hearing things read aloud," Tolkien remembered in 1967, "a power of memory for things received in that way, and also a facility in extempore criticism, none of which were shared (especially not the last) in anything like the same degree by his friends." Lewis, however, did not employ the term "Inklings" in print until his first personal letter written to Charles Williams, dated March 11, 1936. Four years later, Lewis dedicated his 1940 theological tract, *The Problem of Pain*, to the Inklings. By the fall of 1949, the Inklings—by whatever measure—had played itself out as a specific, albeit always fluid, group. When, on October 27, 1949, not a single person showed up to the meeting, the group as group effectively ended.

From roughly 1931 to 1949, however, this group met fairly regularly: on Tuesday afternoons at the Oxford pub, the Eagle and the Child (aka, the Bird and the Baby), and on Thursday evenings in C. S. Lewis's rooms at Oxford. The Inklings first appeared in print, though not by that name, in Chad Walsh's 1949 biography and analysis, *C. S. Lewis: Apostle to the Skeptics*. "The stretch of time from 11:00 to 1:00 on Tuesday mornings Lewis ordinarily manages to keep free so that he can join a small circle of close friends at a certain small, sedate pub," Walsh recorded.

There, in a private parlor, he and the half-a-dozen others pass an hour or two conversing on everything from the nature of God to the latest University events. This particular group dates back to the war years when the Oxford University Press (whose headquarters are normally in London!) fled from the blitz to Oxford, and one of its staff, Charles Williams, became the center of a little circle which met Tuesday mornings at the pub and Thursday evenings in Lewis's college rooms. Charles Williams died in 1945, but the Tuesday morning meetings continue. The group is a fluctuating one. It is likely to contain a couple of Lewis's colleagues such as Professor Tolkien, one or two students, sometimes a relative of someone or a distant friend.

The sheer scope and content of the meetings astounded Walsh.

Only in retrospect did I realize how much intellectual ground was covered in these seemingly casual meetings. At the time the constant bustle of Lewis racing his friends to refill empty mugs or pausing to light another cigarette (occasionally a pipe) camouflaged the steady flow of ideas. The flow, I might add, is not a one-way traffic. Lewis is as good a listener as talker.

In 1947, in *Essays Presented to Charles Williams*, C. S. Lewis described the Inklings as a group of "literary friends . . . we smoked, talked, argued, and drank together." John Wain, a student member of the Inklings, described the group in a similar manner in his 1962 autobiography, *Sprightly Running*. Wain wrote that the Inklings were "a circle of investigators, almost of incendiaries, meeting to urge one another on in the task of redirecting the whole current of contemporary art and life." Further, Wain argued, C. S. Lewis—whom he labeled a "dramatic personality"—led the group as a pro-Christian political cell [Lewis, by the way, adamantly disagreed with this assessment].

Warnie, C. S. Lewis's older brother, remembered the evenings well:

Properly speaking it [The Inklings] was neither a club nor a literary society, but partook of the nature of both. There were no rules, officers, agenda, or formal elections, unless one accepts as a rule the fact that we met in Jack's rooms every Thursday evening after dinner. Proceeding neither began nor terminated at a fixed hour, though there was a tacit agreement that ten-thirty was as late as one could decently arrive. From time to time we added to our original number, but without formalities. Someone would suggest that Jones be asked to come in on a Thursday, and either there would be general agreement or if the suggestion was received with a certain lack of enthusiasm the matter would be dropped. But it was rarely that a name was put forward that was not generally acceptable, for all of us, like Jack himself, knew the sort of man we wanted—and did not want.... The ritual of an Inklings was unvarying. When half a dozen or so had arrived, tea would be produced, after which when pipes were alight Jack would say, "well has nobody got anything to read us?" Out would come a manuscript and we would settle down to sit in judgement upon it. Real, unbiased judgement too, for about the Inklings there was nothing of a mutual admiration society; with us, praise for good work was unstinted but censure for bad, or even not so good, was often brutally frank. To read to the Inklings was a formidable ordeal, and I can still remember the fear and trembling with which I offered the first chapter of my first book—and remember too my delight at its reception.

To be sure, the Inklings were not a mutual admiration society. Somewhat infamously, once when Tolkien pulled out a new chapter of *The Lord of the Rings*, another Inkling gasped, "Oh, fudge, not another elf." Except he didn't say "fudge."

This raises the question, just how important was Lewis to the Inklings? While no one could or should rightly deny the extraordinary influence of Lewis's personality and charisma on the Inklings, stating that "without Lewis's influence, the Inklings would not have been" is simplistic. Two other major factors—and a whole host of smaller ones—contributed to the makeup, ideas, and purpose of the Inklings. The first, though not necessarily in importance, was the publication of Owen Barfield's 1928 work *Poetic Diction*. Written originally as a thesis to earn his B.Litt., Barfield's book exerted a profound influence on the Inklings. In it, Barfield followed Plato's ideas of "divine madness," arguing that not only did imagination allow one to understand his sense data, but also that men "do not *invent* those mysterious relations between separate external objects, and between objects and feelings, which it is the function of poetry to reveal." Instead, Barfield continued, "these relations exist independently, not indeed of Thought, but of any individual thinker." Further, men,

> in the development of consciousness, have lost the power to see this one as one. Our sophistication, like Odin's, has cost us an eye; and now it is the language of poets, in so far as they create true metaphors, which must *restore* this unity conceptually, after it has been lost from perception. Thus, the "before-unapprehended" relationships of which Shelley spoke are in a sense "forgotten" relationships. For though they were never yet apprehended, they were at one time seen. And imagination can see them again.

Barfield, therefore, held the poet's as one of the most important offices in western civilization. Without the development of poetry and the recognition of the necessity of the poet, the western world would become lost in scientistic nominalism and pragmatism and the organic unity of the West would be lost, perhaps permanently. Brilliantly argued, Barfield's *Poetic Diction* falls neatly into the work of a number of important Christian humanist thinkers of the 1920s: that of Nicholas Berdyaev, T. S. Eliot, Christopher Dawson, and Paul Elmer More.

As mentioned above, the influence of Barfield's thought and works upon the various members of the Inklings cannot be exaggerated. In many ways, *Poetic Diction* set the tone for the Inklings, as they saw themselves, as Wain best put it, "redirecting the whole current of contemporary life and art," and myth, metaphor, and poetry would lead the revival. Tolkien may have been the most profoundly influenced, though he had already arrived at many of the same conclusions as Barfield. *Poetic Diction* allowed Tolkien to order and shape his not fully formed thoughts. In a letter to Barfield, Lewis wrote:

> You might like to know that when Tolkien dined with me the other night he said *a propos* of something quite different that your conception of the ancient semantic unity had modified his whole outlook and that he was always just going to say something in a lecture when your conception stopped him in time.

Barfield held a strong affinity for Tolkien's notions on myth as well. And, though the atheist Lewis of the 1920s had fought vehemently against Barfield's Platonic metaphysical ideas, as a Christian, Lewis embraced them, at least in part. One can readily see the influence of Barfield on Lewis in his space trilogy, especially in the first volume, *Out of the Silent Planet.*

The other major influence came from Tolkien's legendarium. Tolkien first presented the manifestations of the mythology—*The Hobbit*, written in the early to mid 1930s, and *The Lord of the Rings*, written between 1938 and 1949—to the Inklings, reading them aloud, chapter by chapter. While each of these things may individually be mere temporal coincidences, the coincidences collectively are too strong to be dismissed. Tolkien met Lewis when he had completed the first major outline of *The Silmarillion*, and the two served together as members of the Koalbiters, which evolved, for the most part, into the Inklings, and the Inklings met until 1949, when Tolkien completed *The Lord of the Rings*. Indeed, Tolkien's mythology served as both a backdrop and a centerpiece for the Inklings.

Still, there were a significant number of other members of this fluid group, and they should never be discounted: C.S. Lewis's brother, historian Warnie; romantic theologian Charles Williams; biographer Lord David Cecil; Royal Naval officer Jim Dundas-Grant; ancient historian C.E. Stevens; the Dominican priest and scholar of Byzantium Mathew Gervase; classicist Colin Hardie; literary scholar Hugo Dyson; physician Robert Havard; historian and political theorist R.B. McCallum; literary scholar Neville Coghill; Anglo-Saxonist C.L. Wrenn; and poet and theologian Adam Fox.

Sometimes students would attend as well, though their role is unclear in the larger history of the Inklings. Regardless, each student who attended offers a fascinating take on what he saw and what it might have meant. These included Christopher Tolkien, J.A.W. Bennett, George Sayers, Roger Lancelyn-Green, and John Wain. Because Dorothy Sayers contributed to the memorial volume written for Charles Williams, some commentators have suggested she, too, was an Inkling. She never was, however. The Inklings remained strictly male during the entirety of its existence.

Again, though, it is critical to remember that the meeting times as well as the membership of the Inklings were always and ever fluid. The group of friends never pretended to be a formal club, and it never desired to exist as a sort of ideological cell. As Lewis cautioned in January 1963, shortly before his death, "The whole picture of myself as one forming a cabinet, or cell, or coven [remember, John Wain's view] is erroneous." To claim such a thing, he noted with adamancy, is to mistake "purely personal relationships for alliances." In other words, to understand the Inklings, one must think apolitically and non-ideologically. One should not see them as promoting any specific man-made ideal or political, cultural, or economic or social system.

Yet a number of things can be stated about the Inklings as a whole. First, the Inklings saw themselves as bardic defenders of the best of western civilization. One only has to think of the numerous passages from *The Lord of the Rings* and *The Silmarillion*, all of which praise the best of the West while never failing to recognize its many sins and sinful longings. The Inklings remained patriotic while also recognizing that true patriotism demands critique, restraint, and self-censorship. The profound Anglo-Welsh man of letters Christopher Dawson remarked in his Gifford Lectures of the late 1940s that the bard—by whatever name or title—stood at the very center of every community, culture, or civilization. He (or she) spoke with the voice of the divine through the poetic and the prophetic, thus acting as an intermediary and a bridge between a god and his worshippers in community. When absent, so too is its representative culture or civilization. There is, of course, a deeply mystical, humanistic, and anti-rationalist impulse in such an ideal. It has the feel of Socrates and Plato all over it. Yet, far from arrogant in its meaning, such an impulse is deeply humbling as well as deeply burdensome. Only through story can a community understand itself, inherit its just rewards, and pass on its wisdom to the next generation, hoping against all odds that that future generation will embrace and transmit the wisdom of ages, on and on. To break the chain serves as the height of arrogance and presumption, whether by an individual, a community, or a generation—what Barfield and Lewis called "chronological snobbery."

Here, then, one might readily see the Inklings as members of a poetic as well as a prophetic community. There are equal parts Plato and Jeremiah in the group, and one finds throughout their works— whether the fiction of Tolkien and Lewis or the biographies of Lord

David Cecil—thorough, wide, and deep discussions of dreaming, poetry, imagination, visions, and mystical experiences. Lewis and Tolkien each believed in personal forms of mystical experience, but they also imbued their fictional characters with these same attributes. The physical senses matter, to be sure, but the soul and the imagination matter even more. Each considered beauty, properly understood, as a contextualization of hope. Beyond this, the bard should touch upon the meaning, heroism, beauty, holiness, and sanctity, while never forgetting the more mundane things such as style, context, and presentation. The bard expresses all of these longings with whatever gifts have been given to him and to the community, whether those of the community possess the ears, the will, or the integrity to hear and understand or not.

One might readily think of Aragorn telling the tale of Beren and Lúthien, only moments before the Ringwraiths attack at Weathertop. Still a stranger to his companions at that point in the story, Aragorn serves here as the bard, but his tale has as much in common with prayer as it does with mere taletelling. Indeed, could one even imagine *The Lord of the Rings* absent its myriad of songs? Each connects the singer to something historical and significant, not only binding together the immediate group, but tying that group to something larger. Even the seemingly homely songs of Sam bind the company to the hearth and home of the Shire.

Second, the various Inklings took seriously the ideas and realities of friendship as a necessary bulwark against the dread conformity of the modern, western free world, what Alexis de Tocqueville called "democratic despotism," and that of the East, totalitarianism. Here, again, one must think in pre- or a-ideological terms. A true friendship, by its very nature, is exclusive but non-political. "That outlook which values the collective above the individual necessarily disparages Friendship; it is a relation between men at their highest level of individuality," Lewis wrote in 1960's *The Four Loves*. "It withdraws men from collective 'togetherness' as surely as solitude itself could do; and more dangerously, for it withdraws them by two's and three's."

Yet we must not think of "the crowd" and then "the Inklings." Instead, as Lewis and Tolkien understood it, a free and properly functioning world meant that millions upon millions of communities existed, some overlapping, some not. An individual person belongs not just to one such community at any given time in his or her life, but rather to many. Time and circumstance, as much as personal desire and loyalty, shape the time and treasure a person gives to each association to which he belongs.

And whatever opposition the world offered, friendship was worth it. Throughout Tolkien's academic as well as fictional writings, he stresses again and again the necessity of friendship and community. In some of his earliest tales, not surprisingly, Tolkien began his stories in a room or hall, with all of the characters seated around a fire. The fire that warmed the hearts of the bards as well as the audience he called the "Tale-fire" in the posthumously published *Book of Lost Tales*. A similar place existed in the house of Elrond, in *The Hobbit* and *The Lord of the Rings*. On a much more personal level, Tolkien had always belonged to some group of friends that dedicated itself to some mission or calling. Prior to the war, Tolkien had experienced an incredible and meaningful friendship with three others in his school, King Edward's: Christopher Wiseman, Geoffrey Smith, and Rob Gilson. The best of friends, they had called themselves the TCBS, the Tea Club and Barrovian Society. They stayed close to one another after graduating, holding periodic "Councils" to share poetry and ideas.

Gilson died on July 1, 1916, at the Somme. Shaken, Tolkien wrote that the three remaining had a duty, a duty to achieve greatness, not for personal glory, but for God's glory, to be a "great instrument in God's hands." Just as Gilson had achieved greatness through his sacrifice for something greater than himself, so the remaining three friends must be "steeped with the same holiness of courage, suffering and sacrifice." Tolkien considered July 1 a holy day, to be remembered for the rest of their lives. So he wrote Smith on August 12. Sometime in the week before Christmas of that year, Tolkien received a letter from Wiseman. German shrapnel had taken the life of Smith. Now, only two remained. "Of course the TCBS may have been all we dreamt," Tolkien had written in that letter to Smith, "and its work in the end to be done by three or two or one survivor and the part of the others be trusted by God to that of the inspiration which we do know we all got and get from one another." These words must have echoed in Tolkien's mind and soul as he pondered the death of Smith.

Lewis, too, wrote openly about the necessity of friendship and exclusion. "Friendship is the greatest of worldly goods," Lewis claimed in a personal letter. "Certainly to me it is the chief happiness of life. If I had to give a piece of advice to a young man about a place to live, I think I should say, 'sacrifice almost everything to live where you can be near your friends.'"

Third, the Inklings were extraordinary at making the good good. They did this through myth (poetic myth at that) itself. Tolkien lectured to an academic audience at the University of St. Andrews in the late 1930s, saying:

> We may indeed be older now, in so far as we are heirs in enjoyment or in practice of many generations of ancestors in the arts. In this inheritance of wealth there may be a danger of boredom or of anxiety to be original, and that may lead to a distaste for fine drawing, delicate pattern, and "pretty" colours, or else to mere manipulation and over-elaboration of old material, clever and heartless. We should look at green again, and be startled anew (but not blinded) by blue and yellow and red. We should meet the centaur and the dragon, and then perhaps suddenly behold, like ancient shepherds, sheep, dogs, and horses—and wolves.

Further, why should one protest the so-called "escape" that literature and mythology provide, Tolkien asked?

> For it is after all possible for a rational man, after reflection (quite unconnected with fairy-story or romance), to arrive at the condemnation, implicit at least in the mere silence of "escapist" literature, of progressive things like factories, or the machine-guns and bombs that appear to be their most natural and inevitable, dare we say "inexorable," products.

One can also think of Tolkien's description of Gandalf in *The Silmarillion*. Gandalf, known as Olorin in the True West, had been the least of the Istari sent to Middle-earth to aid Men and Elves in their war against Sauron. Though the least powerful, he was the wisest, and he spent many of his days walking among the Elves "unseen, or in a form as one of them, and they did not know whence came the fair visions or the promptings of wisdom that he put into their hearts." *The Silmarillion* records that "those who listened to him awoke from despair and put away the imaginations of darkness."

Lewis also admired the art of escape through poetry, literature, and the imagination. "The Fantastic or Mythical is a Mode available at all ages for some readers; for others, at none. At all ages, if it is well used by the author and meets the right reader, it has the same power," Lewis wrote for the *New York Times* in 1956, "to generalise while remaining concrete, to present in palpable form not concepts or even experiences but whole classes of experience, and to throw off irrelevancies." In its best form, the fantastic can "add to" life, not just "comment on" it.

In his 1928 book *Poetic Diction*, Owen Barfield had written: civilization "must look more and more to art—to the individualized poet—as the very source and fountain-head of *all* meaning." In a 1984 interview, Barfield nicely summed up the thinking of Lewis and Tolkien on art and literature: all "felt that literature shouldn't be used as a means of propagating a message." Further, he noted, "the thing that mattered was that it was a good work of art, and that had its own value, which in the long run was a Christian value. I think that that would perhaps be as fair a way as I could imagine of stating both Tolkien's and Lewis's attitude."

Fourth, and related to the first point, the Inklings as a whole viewed themselves and their group as making a final, noble, and romantic defense of the Old West. Lewis, in his Cambridge Inaugural Address of 1954, described himself as a dinosaur, one of the last "Old Western Men."

> It is my settled conviction that in order to read Old Western literature aright you must suspend most of the responses and unlearn most of the habits you have acquired in reading modern literature. And because this is the judgement of a native, I claim that, even if the defence of my conviction is weak, the fact of my conviction is a historical datum to which you should give full weight. That way, where I fail as a critic, I may yet be useful as a specimen. I would even dare to go further. Speaking not only for myself but for all other Old Western men whom you may meet, I would say, use your specimens while you can. There are not going to be many more dinosaurs.

Clyde Kilby, an Evangelical from Wheaton College who wrote about Lewis and also worked closely with Tolkien on *The Silmarillion* during the summer of 1966, explained:

> Like Lewis, Tolkien was an Old Western Man who was staggered at the present direction of civilization. Even our much vaunted talk of equality he felt debased by our attempts to "mechanize and formalize it." Equality he believed to be primarily spiritual, not simply a moral, affair. Like Lewis, he regarded any evolutionary change as downward, not upward.

While Tolkien saw evil in 1916, he also saw it in 1969. "The spirit of wickedness in high places is now so powerful and so many-headed in its incarnations," Tolkien wrote, "that there seems nothing more to do than personally to refuse to worship any of the hydras' heads." The world, he explained in an interview in the mid-1960s, seemed little better than a new Tower of Babel, "all noise and confusion." It would be difficult for a conservative and traditionalist such as Tolkien to have viewed the world in any other way. In addition to recognizing the effects of original sin in all eras and over all humans, Tolkien found the twentieth century especially troubling and downright horrifying. Tolkien had lamented the rise of what he and his friends called the machine, mechanizing life, dulling and conforming it, draining it of its vitality. The machine had appeared in a variety of forms. Democratic governments had bureaucratized the beauty out of language on the more benign end of the political continuum. At the other end, fascistic and communist ideologues had raped, plundered, murdered, and dehumanized entire populations, massacring upwards of 200,000,000 persons in the century.

Again, it is vital to understand the Inklings not in ideological terms, but in poetic and romantic terms. "The stance of a last survivor always attracted" Lewis, one of the youngest Inklings, J. A. W. Bennett, remembered. "It is one of the likings he shared with William Morris, and it early drew him to the sagas and the doomed Eddaic gods." Whether it was through epic fantasies, science fiction, philosophy, or biography, the Inklings stood as a little platoon defending what would soon be lost utterly and completely to the world. The effort, no matter the cost or the result, remained the everlasting goal. Should fame or acknowledgement come to any or all of them was certainly fine, but it was fine only in that it promoted the whole and the message of the whole. "I don't think Lewis and I were much 'worried' about the possibility of not becoming great men," Barfield recalled in an interview given ten years after Lewis's death. They had their duty, and they would fulfill that duty no matter the cost and no matter how many or how few voices listened to them. As Tolkien put it, they were fighting the "Long Defeat."

To conclude, we should note that in a Platonic sense, the Inklings might very well have brought about an *anamnesis*, a remembering of what had been lost, but they might also very well have been simply preservers of timeless wisdom for many ages to come, so far into the future as to seem unimaginable. Through their efforts, they might bring some back to first principles, reforming what had gone wrong in society. As the Inklings well knew, Socrates, Plato, and Aristotle came at the end and in the aftermath of fallen classical Greece; Cicero and Cato the Younger appeared at the end of the Roman republic; St. Augustine at the end of the Roman Empire; and Dante at the end of the Medieval. Each of these profound western men came at a moment in which they could imagine, ideally, what had come before them and pray that someone in the future would remember what was so rapidly being lost in their own day and age. So it was, most likely, with the Inklings.

Romance After Tolkien?

If you look at what's playing on your television, at what's showing at the local cinema, at what video games your children are playing, or at what is selling in the young adult section of your neighborhood Barnes and Nobles, you'll see something that is at once deeply cultural and deeply counter-cultural. Romanticism. It's everywhere, and it's at once beloved and vilified by the society that has so embraced it.

In academia, not surprisingly, social scientists despise it. It's all airy nonsense, just "make believe," they claim when they think of the matter at all. At best, it's a useful diversion for the young and uneducated, and, at worst, it's an unhealthy and anti-social dose of non-reality.

The American public, though, seems to feel differently.

One of the most startling and piercing artistic movements of the past two and one-half centuries has been romanticism. It's difficult to know exactly where the movement started, though most historians and literary scholars would give the nod to Edmund Burke and his second great work, *On the Sublime and the Beautiful.* From Burke's treatise, almost all modern Romantic thought arose. Burke's presence is at times implicit and at times blatant in the works of such critical figures as Wordsworth and Coleridge, but it can be found throughout most of the romantic poetry and art of the early nineteenth century. It's not hard even to imagine Burke's shadow lingering over Beethoven's Sixth Symphony, the "Pastoral." In his own writings on western civilization, Christopher Dawson argued that the rise of Romanticism, whatever its excesses and failings, was as important to western civilization as the re-discovery of Hellenic thought in the Renaissance. Whatever its original and essential intent, Romanticism successfully saved Christianity from the utilitarianism and rationalism of the eighteenth century, Dawson continued. In its recovery of medieval Christianity in the early nineteenth century, the Anglo-Welsh Roman Catholic scholar asserted that the Romantics actually discovered "a new kind of beauty."

Romance After Tolkien?

From its earliest origins, one can trace Romanticism's history through the nineteenth century and into the early twentieth century through figures as diverse as Friedrich Nietzsche, G. K. Chesterton, and Willa Cather. Perhaps most important for western culture, however, was its manifestation in the vast mythology of J. R. R. Tolkien.

Not surprisingly, especially given its origins in the thought of Edmund Burke, Romanticism, properly understood, is deeply conservative in its praise of the ancestors, its idealization of the past, and its admiration of folk customs as a greater wisdom than any one generation or one person can know. Romanticism is also, properly understood, deeply sacramental. Like all good things in this world, it can be perverted to varying degrees. Its love of the past and one's ancestry can be unthinkingly reactionary, its love of place can become pantheistic, and its love of the folk can become nationalistic and even, at times, downright fascistic.

In the twentieth century, as noted above, the greatest expression of a proper Romanticism can be found in the works of J. R. R. Tolkien as well as in the works of the other Inklings, C. S. Lewis, Owen Barfield, and Lord David Cecil. In terms of sales and influence, however, Tolkien has far exceeded that of his closest friends. For almost anyone under the age of 55, Tolkien is a champion of great art and high imagination. For an older generation—in general—he still, unfortunately, represents decadent hippiness, magic mushrooms, and psychedelic tuning out.

Fundamentalists of all ages also fear Tolkien, too, worrying that his discussion of magic and elves and dwarves is somehow a bit too dark and unchristian, perhaps created with noble intent, but the devil's work, nonetheless. After all, it was the Tolkien craze that spawned (or at least radically increased) the popularity of such games as *Dungeons and Dragons* and such music as *Led Zeppelin IV*. Once the province of nerds and nerds only, *Dungeons and Dragons* has become powerfully mainstream, and as various scholars have argued, one can trace a rather direct line from Tolkien to *D&D* to modern video games. And Led Zeppelin's music is now as much a part of western civilization as is Beethoven, though often relegated to the wallpaper sounds of Muzak in our elevators of commerce and industry.

Assuming, fair reader, that you are not worried that you might lose your soul when listening to "Stairway to Heaven" or that demons lurk when spending an evening with friends pretending to be an elf as you roll the dice in some distant imaginary land, you might very well be curious as to what is good in this huge and Romantic bent in fiction over the past century. Tolkien and Lewis, to be sure. But what about that great question, "and, after Tolkien?" If you're asking yourself this—for you or your kids or grandkids— you're not alone. As someone who has had the grand privilege of spending much of his academic career studying Tolkien, fantasy, and science fiction, I often get asked, "OK, after Tolkien, now what?"

It should be noted that there is a lot of mediocre literature for sale in Barnes and Noble (and all other fine book retailers). Indeed, there exists far more mediocre ("the OK") than diabolic or good. In this discussion, I'll avoid the mediocre completely. Be hot or cold, but "lukewarm, get away from me!" As to the diabolic, there are three authors that serious lovers of Romantic literature should avoid: Philip Pullman, Michael Moorcock, and Stephen Donaldson, each of whom has intentionally set out to undermine, subvert, and pervert the Christian elements of Tolkienian fantasy. They are, to put it mildly, not only anti-Christian and anti-romantic, but painfully so. They are, to be sure, quite talented, but they use their talents in ways that undermine the very gifts of truth, beauty, and goodness.

As I list what to read "after Tolkien," I must make two caveats. First, almost no one has reached the literary quality of Tolkien's writings, whether in his clever children's stories, such as *The Hobbit*, or in his high fantasy, such as in *The Lord of the Rings* and *The Silmarillion*. And, second, no one has reached the imaginative quality of Tolkien's writings, either. For better or worse, these two must be givens as we consider "after Tolkien." And these two might be givens for the next several centuries.

Of all twentieth-century fabulists, Ray Bradbury comes closest to equaling Tolkien's literary and imaginative powers. Unlike his English counterpart, however, Bradbury excelled in the direct, sharp, and well-defined story. There is no meandering in a Bradbury story, no extraordinary quest, no prolonged journey. Bradbury would latch fiercely onto one idea or one image and write a short story around that one thing. "Life is short, misery sure, mortality certain," Bradbury noted in the early 1970s. "But on the way, in your work, why not carry these two inflated pigbladders labeled Zest and Gusto." He was a master of these two pigbladders, and even his novels—such as *Martian Chronicles* and *Fahrenheit 451*—are really just compilations of short stories. One of Bradbury's best novels, as well as his most neglected, is his story of good and evil as represented and manifested in two young boys, *Something Wicked This Way Comes*. It might very well be the best Christian book written by a non-Christian in the twentieth century.

If she had taken two or even three times longer to write her seven books of the Harry Potter series, Scottish authoress J.K. Rowling might have achieved a form of literary immortality. As they are, the Harry Potter books are extremely clever and relentlessly entertaining, but they will probably not be read a century from now. Some newer, more clever series will have taken its place by then. Still, for what they are—despite the worries of fundamentalist Catholics— the Harry Potter books are both pro-western civilization and pro- Catholic. Well versed in the western canon, Rowling peppers her stories with a vast amount of specifically Catholic symbolism: the blood of the unicorn bringing everlasting death upon those unwor- thy to drink of it; the rebirth of the phoenix named, ironically enough, Fawkes (Guy Fawkes was a seventeenth-century Roman Catholic terrorist lampooned by British Protestants); the use of a variety of saints names such as Hedwig, Mungo, and Brutus; the communion of saints in the form of Harry's family in his first direct battle with Voldemort in a graveyard. And this is just a short list. Perhaps most tellingly, the wizards became illegal and had to form recusant communities in 1689, the very same year (in reality) that Catholics had to do so in Britain.

For those of a certain age, Terry Brooks will always be remem- bered for writing his Shannara trilogy in the late 1970s and early 1980s. Brooks openly borrowed from Tolkien, and, at the time, the critics lambasted him even as thousands upon thousands of kids devoured his books, eagerly hoping to find more adventures of romantic heroes. Since the early 1980s, the Shannara universe has grown brilliantly, and Brooks—rather open about his own Protestant Christianity—has grown equally brilliantly as a writer. As with much of fantasy (and some Protestantism), Brooks too often veers into Manicheanism, but, then again, so did St. Augustine. His universe is based on a seemingly never-ending war of the Word and the Void. The Word seeks to leaven all life, while the Void seeks nothing but annihilation. Far from the winding sentences and paragraphs of the first few Shannara books, the more recent ones are pithy, honed, and direct. As with Tolkien, Brooks does an excellent job exploring the good of good while not basking in the evil of evil.

Though remembered more for his nonfiction such as *The Conservative Mind* and *Roots of American Order*, Russell Kirk produced some of the most powerful fiction of the last century. In terms of his short stories, one might very well imagine the power of a Bradbury with the morality of a Flannery O'Connor. These, too, deal with good and evil, though Kirk is at his best when describing noble sacrifices. His best book, however, is a dark but powerfully Christian fantasy called *The Lord of the Hollow Dark*. In it, Kirk places all of the major figures from the plays and poems of T. S. Eliot at a Scottish castle dedicated to Satanism and the performance of a black Mass. Not surprisingly, the dialogue is intellectually rigorous while the plot remains riveting. It is a rare achievement of high philosophy, fantasy, and theology and deserves a much wider audience than it has thus far received.

Sharing the same literary agent, Stephen King took inspiration from Kirk, strangely enough. While they have different views politically, the two men saw good and evil in much the same way, and each reveres place (Michigan, Scotland, Maine) in a way usually reserved for the most traditionalist of traditionalists. The great difference between the two authors, of course, is that King wallows in the decadence and immorality of evil, though he is equally good at evoking the good and the heroic. Whereas Kirk might allude to a murder, for example, King gives us five to six pages of gruesome description of that murder. Five such pages can readily change the entire tone of a novel. King's best novel—in terms of literary quality and imaginative power—is *Salem's Lot*, a rewrite of Bram Stoker's *Dracula* set in small-town Maine.

Best known for his Hugo-nominated science-fiction novels and young adult fiction (*Star Wars*, in particular), Kevin J. Anderson has written a number of wonderful fantasy novels. His best, however, is the *Terra Incognita* series, a three-volume story based on the claims of the sea, a sort-of Frank Herbert's *Dune*, but set in water rather than sand. Overall, Anderson's good characters tend to be more gray than those of Tolkien or Bradbury, but he rarely if ever explores the nuances of evil, preferring to put his energies in the creation of deep characters and intricate plots.

Two authors I find as perplexing as I do fascinating are Katherine Kurtz and Stephen Lawhead. When at their best, they are each extremely good. Kurtz, a trained medievalist, has created an entire universe (Deryni) based on an idealized late medieval, Catholic Wales. The Deryni are similar to humans, but they possess magic. The Church, understandably, knows not what to make of all of this. Kurtz, to her credit, deals openly with questions of magic and grace, miracle, and sacrament. Though a convert to Roman Catholicism, she has left the Church for what is called "Celtic Christianity."

Though never Catholic, evangelical author Stephen Lawhead also considers himself a Celtic Christian. At his best, Lawhead is amazing. At his worst, he's dreadful. His best work, which should be regarded as a classic, is his six-volume story about King Arthur. Giving the Celtic rather than the more accepted French version of the story, Lawhead successfully mixes classical gods, demigods, and heroes with Atlantean dreams and Christian theology. It's quite a feat, but Lawhead performs it well. The six volumes revolve around the dream of Taliessen, known as the "Kingdom of Summer."

> There is a land, a land of shining goodness where each man protects his brother's dignity as readily as his own, where war and want have ceased and all tribes live under the same law of love and honor. It is a land bright with truth, where a man's word is his pledge and falsehood is banished, where children sleep safe in their mother's arms and never know fear or pain. It is a land where kings extend their hands in justice rather than reach for the sword; where mercy, kindness, and compassion flow like deep water, and where men revere virtue, revere truth, revere beauty above comfort, pleasure or selfish gain. A land where peace reigns in the

hearts of men. Where faith blazes like a beacon from every hill and love like a fire from every hearth; where the True God is worshipped and His ways acclaimed by all.

Certainly, there is no better introduction to the Arthurian mythology than Lawhead's.

Before concluding this chapter, I must make one other note. When you're perusing books at Barnes and Noble, Books-A-Million, or Half-Price Books, you'll see a section in Sci-Fi/Fantasy called "Series." In this section, you'll find everything from novelizations of Batman movies to Star Trek novels to video name novelizations. For years, I glided past these, dismissing the novels as nothing more than pulp trash. I really could have not been more incorrect in my assessment. A number of serial authors—such as Josh Vogt, R. A. Salvatore, and Tracy Hickman—are quite good. Rather than dismissing these authors as pulp writers, we might just as readily see them as world-builders, allowing for a deep examination of a time and a place in their settings.

In the end, it's well worth quoting Tolkien's praise of such literature.

For it is after all possible for a rational man, after reflection (quite unconnected with fairy-story or romance), to arrive at the condemnation, implicit at least in the mere silence of "escapist" literature, of progressive things like factories, or the machine-guns and bombs that appear to be their most natural and inevitable, dare we say "inexorable," products.

If one is forced to choose between dropping an atomic bomb on the Christian city of Nagasaki or wielding a sword in the romantic defense of the Church, the choice is clear.

Science Fiction: Existence Before Definition

Do you want to rule a world? Blow apart a sun? Test a theory of community? Explore the very depths of depravity? End slavery and misery? Destroy all empires?

It's possible... At least in the imagination. "The proper study of man is everything. The proper study of man as artist is everything which gives a foothold to the imagination and the passions" (C.S. Lewis, "On Science Fiction").

As it surrounds us now and resides, specifically, in no medium, we take science fiction for granted. Though we have lost the "new frontier" aspect of science fiction as exploration of other worlds, we have certainly thrown ourselves into exploring the limits—at least technologically and scientifically—of this one. I'm typing this on a gadget that Steve Jobs imagined even better than did Star Trek and its "futurism."

During the first half of the twentieth century, however, what came to be known as science fiction was nothing short of disreputable to almost all literati and to the American public at large. It was considered low-class as well as, contradictorily, childish and quasi-pornographic. Associated with pulp, science fiction books usually appeared on drug store shelves next to ribald sex stories, romances, and comic books. Aside from a few prominent novels—such as *Brave New World*—science fiction remained suspect to most but highly regarded to a few. Those few could be truly fanatic and evangelical, meeting at various times of the year at what would become known as conventions, writing and mailing newsletters, and trading books and novels whenever possible. The detective/mystery author Sharon McCrumb has written two mysteries set at early science fiction conventions, and, at least to this author, nailed the culture perfectly.

All of this shunning and disreputability, however, served the new genre well as it grew mightily and without the restrictions that mainstream publishing placed on so much of the fiction of the time, especially in New York, where neither Jews nor Catholics were much welcomed in respectable publishing. Decentralized and unconnected to any single urban center, science fiction writers could be anti-ideological, anti-conformity, and subversive of WASPish norms. They could explore any thing, any setting, and any personality or community in any situation or setting. Truly, the possibilities were endless. Geniuses such as C. S. Lewis, Ray Bradbury, Isaac Asimov, Alfred Bester, and Robert Heinlein found themselves at the center of a new movement, one that allowed for the flourishing of imagination. Through their own speculations about what could be, science fiction also witnessed a grand critiquing of what was—especially in response to the rise of totalitarian and terrorist ideologies.

Before "science fiction" became the go-to term for the genre, those in favor and those against employed other names and terms such as "fabulist," "speculative fiction," "pseudoscience fiction," and "scientifiction." Frankly, these terms serve just as well as the one that became the norm, and each reveals the expansiveness and possibilities of such literature. During the 1950s, though, Lewis, Bradbury, and Sam Moskowitz promoted the concept of science fiction. As the term only slowly became acceptable (mostly as it became profitable), the literati trashed science fiction for its supposedly childish desire to escape. As Lewis so cuttingly responded:

> That perhaps is why people are so ready with the charge of "escape." I never fully understood it till my friend Professor Tolkien asked me the very simple question, "What class of men would you expect to be most preoccupied with, and most hostile to, the idea of escape?" and gave the obvious answer: jailers. The charge of Fascism is, to be sure, mere mud-flinging. Fascists, as well as Communists, are jailers; both would assure us that the proper study of prisoners is prison. But there is perhaps this truth behind it: that those who brood much on the remote past or future, or stare long at the night sky, are less likely than others to be ardent or orthodox partisans. ("On Science Fiction")

In the post-modern world of inhumane horrors—all quite real— what sane person would not want to escape?

As Lewis understood it, the literati only wanted to comment on life's banality and dreariness, while those who love science fiction want to dream dreams. For every realist in New York City, perhaps, two romantics lurked in the fields of Illinois or in the pubs of Oxford.

Science Fiction at the University of Chicago

During the spring semester of 1957, the University of Chicago invited a number of distinguished speakers to campus to lecture on the meaning and significance of science fiction as a genre. Robert Heinlein, C.M. Kornbluth, Robert Bloch, and Alfred Bester each gave insightful speeches, all of which were collected by Basil Davenport and published in his collection *The Science Fiction Novel: Imagination and Social Criticism*. This was one of the first times that anyone—aside from the efforts of C.S. Lewis, Ray Bradbury, and Sam Moskowitz—had attempted at any systematic level to define the admittedly elusive concept of science fiction.

The very term "science fiction," though first employed in the second half of the 1920s, had only recently become an accepted label. "Extraordinary voyages," "scientific romances," "scientific fantasies," "off-trail stories," "different stories," "impossible stories," "scientific fiction," "weird scientific stories," "scientifiction," and "scientification" had all competed with it. That the University of Chicago—arguably the greatest university in the world in the 1950s—was attempting to define the genre offered great weight and credibility to it.

The four presenters, though, disagreed with one another profoundly, and several dismissed the label "science fiction" as wrongheaded and misleading. Heinlein, arguably the best known of the presenters and the standard-bearer of the genre, preferred the term "speculative fiction." Regardless, he especially wanted his work to be seen as something quite separate from "fantasy."

"I am not condemning fantasy, I am defining it. It has greater freedom than any other form of fiction, for it is completely independent of the real world and is limited only by literary rules relating to empathy, inner logic and the like," Heinlein claimed, arguing rather directly against J.R.R. Tolkien's beautifully crafted argument for fantasy in 1939. Still, he continued, "its great freedom makes it, in the hands of a skilled craftsman, a powerful tool for entertainment and instruction—humor, satire, gothic horror, anything you wish."

Science fiction, however, had to be rooted in both the possible and the probable, with the rules of engineering, mathematics, chemistry, and biology in play.

> A handy short definition of almost all science fiction might read: realistic speculation about possible future events, based solidly on adequate knowledge of the real world, past and present, and on a thorough understanding of the nature and significance of the scientific method.

Science fiction, as such, is always and everywhere, then, possibly if not probably, prophetic. Sometimes that prophecy is coincidental, but, in many cases, it is transformative, guiding the very evolution and science of a thing. It inspires as well as predicts. The downside to this, Heinlein laments, is that while science fiction writers know science and engineering, they only very rarely know how to write well. Still, Heinlein claimed with no small amount of bias, science fiction is the most important literature in existence, for it is the history of the future rather than the history of the dead past. Even more so, he continued, it runs counter to the dark and perverted pessimism of "realism," which, more often than not, he claimed, is really just a label to cover the psychologically sick and demented, "stuff that should not be printed, but told only privately—on a psychiatrist's couch. . . . I, for one, am heartily sick of stories about frustrates, jerks, homosexuals, and commuters." In science fiction, Heinlein concluded, every social experiment ever conceived can be tested safely, free from actual harm in society. That which works in literature, then, can be implemented, and that which doesn't should remain only on the printed page.

Bitterly, C. M. Kornbluth, the second presenter, vehemently disagreed, stating without equivocation that the genre "is not an important medium of social criticism." Much like Hitler, Kornbluth complained, the adherents of science fiction treat the genre like a religion and lay claim to anything and everything they admire. Yet, for all its pretensions, science fiction rarely if ever actually criticizes anything prevalent in the world, and, when it does, its criticism remains rather tame. Anticipating the social radicals of a decade later, Kornbluth feared that science fiction fails in its power to change the consciousness of a reader, as the novels of the genre do "not turn the reader outward to action but inward to contemplation." Then, he complained, there's the horror genre, a supposed subset of science fiction which merely rolls all of our fears "up in one ball of muck" and thrusts "them into the reader's face." This is especially true in cinema, he continued, and "if the day ever comes when the shriek movie is a really major type, up there with, say, the pretentious Western, the implications for the future of democracy will be bad." Yet one should never give any of this too much thought, he concluded, for "science fiction is socially impotent." Tragically, Kornbluth died a year later, of a heart attack, only age 34.

Author of two of the best science fiction novels of the 1950s—*The Demolished Man* and *The Stars My Destination*—Alfred Bester argued that as the genre is deeply rooted in romanticism, it can serve as a literature that explores all of the goodness of the human person, in a fashion similar to the arguments made in the eighteenth century by Jean-Jacques Rousseau. "I believe that everyone is compelled, but no one is bad. I believe that everyone has greatness in him, but few of us have the opportunity to fulfill ourselves." At this point, Bester is simply anticipating *Star Trek*'s Gene Roddenberry, yet he took his argument into a more theological realm. "I believe that everyone has love in him, but most of our loves are frustrated."

We are also, Bester thought, natural lovers of science fiction because it is a mechanized form of romanticism. "We're a nation of amateur mechanics," he wrote. "We're simpatico to science and invention, and can identify with mechanical genius." After all, he reasoned, at least four out of every five Americans longed to become a famous inventor. Even sitcoms, he continued, appeal to Americans because they are mechanical comedy, based on situation rather than character.

The final presenter, Robert Bloch, most famously the author of *Psycho* (and, thus, exactly the type of science fiction writer that Kornbluth despised), proved to be the most interesting. Contrary to almost everything that Kornbluth had claimed, Bloch argued that science fiction, more than any other genre, offered both the best and the most complex forms of social criticism. After all, in the ability to imagine, the individual is let loose to counter the conformity—in business, in government, in education—so rampant in post-World War II America. As a genre, science fiction allowed authors fully to explore three critical themes: "Man against Nature, Man against Himself and Man against Man."

Still, he cautioned, there's the danger of science fiction merely becoming the repetitive story of the unusual man brought forth to right some mediocre wrong. In these stories, there is the "reassuring Father-Image of the all-wise scientist and psychotherapist. With his aid, the hero triumphs." It is rather difficult for the modern reader not to imagine Obi-Wan Kenobi and Luke Skywalker in Bloch's caution. "Science fiction thus reassures people that they are the masters of their fate, and that every mushroom cloud has a silver lining," he joked.

Whatever its faults, science fiction has the ability to explode all limits and allow us to see the world (and worlds) in a million-plus ways.

While *The Science Fiction Novel* is by no means a perfect book, it is a fascinating one. Most importantly, though, it offers us a brief but powerful glimpse into the role of imagination at the same time and in the same era that conservatives such as Russell Kirk and Robert Nisbet were so vehemently claiming that only imagination will save us from the morally and ethically desiccated ideological forces unleashed by the first two world wars.

The Haunting of Piety Hill, Michigan[1]

I'm especially glad that the Midwestern History Association has chosen to honor Kirk as one of its greats. Truly, he and Bruce Catton represent the very best of Michigan culture, history, and personality. It is especially fitting to honor him at Michigan State, where he earned his B.A. (Class of 1940) and later served as a professor from 1946 through 1953.

My comment deals specifically with the role of sacramental and anti-sacramental soil as found in Mecosta, Michigan, and its environs. At least as Russell Kirk understood this and imagined it. The curtain between the world of the living and of the dead is truly thin for Kirk, in his scholarly work and in his fiction.

"Some mediums are charlatans, but others possess genuine, if inexplicable and dangerous power," Kirk argued in a 1967 newspaper column. "I advise no one to meddle with the next world who is not very strong of mind and heart," he continued. As late as 1973, though, Kirk continued to read the Tarot cards for guests, and he maintained his love of Halloween—"an annual occasion of dreadful joy at my house"—to the end of his life. "Kirk was old hand at telling fortunes by the Tarot, long before the art was taken up by hippies," he wrote of himself in a publicity brochure from the early 1970s. "My fortunes invariably are melancholy, and as invariably come to pass," he believed. From his earliest memories as a child, Kirk believed in ghosts. Having been raised among deracinated Puritans, Spiritualists, and Swedenborgians, he witnessed "that uncanny business" of auto writing, the levitations of great-grandmothers, rocking chairs, playing musical instruments, and tables, visitations from the dead (sometimes in spectral form), and seances as a normal part of his upbringing. "Henry James was a man with Swedenborgian forebears who didn't believe in ghosts; I am one with Swedenborgian forebears who DOES believe in ghosts," Kirk wrote in a private letter to philosopher Eric Voegelin. "Everybody who stays here in my ances-

---

1. This originated as a talk given to the Midwestern History Association.

tral house of Piety Hill becomes a more fervent believer than even I am," he continued. According to Kirk, the ghostly phenomena only increased with the passing of years, until 1975, when the house burned. Consumed by fire, all of the ghosts departed Piety Hill.

For the most part, he lamented, ghosts simply are restless spirits that have not enjoyed the sleep of the just prior to God's final judgment. Exorcism helps the living as much as it frees the dead. Rather than fear ghosts, Kirk claimed, the living should pity them, enabling them to break free of the bonds of this world whenever and wherever possible. "I have no desire for my dear ones to walk the night," he wrote in 1967. "Let them sleep sound, until the Last Trump."

Having grown up with the otherworldly phenomena, Kirk delved deeply into and read extensively the serious literature about the supernatural and the occult. He also investigated a number of claims in the U.S. and in Europe, and he even contributed to at least one serious work of the occult, Brad Steiger's 1969 *Stranger Powers of ESP*. Though he received no authorial credit on the cover of the book, Kirk wrote chapter 2, "A Note on Ghostly Phenomena in Russell Kirk's Old House at Mecosta, Michigan." A belief in the supernatural, he held, served as a marker for our understanding of faith. In an age of faith, the human person took the supernatural as natural. One saw unusual things, and saints radiated, as represented in the "halo" of art. In an age of scientism, the person and the culture dismissed the supernatural event as ridiculous and religion as a whole as superstitious.[2] But, as Kirk put it rather humorously in a 1966 newspaper column, the haunting and haunted spirits of the world, in turn, "simply ignore rationalists." Regardless, he argued, a mass of anecdotal evidences has sprung forth from almost every era

---

2. It should be noted, RAK especially disliked the literary genre of science-fiction, seeing it, in general, as banal and meaningless, a superficial mirroring of the works of H. G. Wells. This is surprising, given how thoughtful writers such as Walter Miller, James Blish, or Kingsley Amis could be, and how much in line they would be with RAK's own understanding of the world. The best science fiction, to RAK's mind, was that of Ray Bradbury and C. S. Lewis, the kind that is far more fantasy set in space than what might be termed hard science fiction. These are, essentially, what literary critic and biographer Joseph Pearce would call "theological thrillers."

and every culture and religion in human history of the appearance of ghosts, revenants, and poltergeists. To ignore all of this, he argued, served as pure obstinacy. "Have I ever seen a ghost? Why, I am one, and so are you—a geist, a spirit, in a mortal envelope," he wrote in 1979.

Kirk's belief went well beyond this clever statement, however. As a child, he encountered two ghostly figures, staring at him from the outside in a blizzard. The taller one, wearing a beard, was Dr. Cady. The shorter, wearing a turban, was Patti. Kirk's Aunt Fay had encountered the same figures as a little girl, and Kirk's daughter, Monica, encountered them as a child as well. Dr. Cady appeared as a real figure, doctor of the paranormal and husband of Yolande, in Kirk's short story "The Princess of All Lands." As a graduate student in Scotland, he saw fairies, goblins, and several ghosts. He was especially taken with one simply known as Captain Gair.

As Kirk believed it, his ancestors haunted Piety Hill until the great fire destroyed it all on Ash Wednesday, 1975. Kirk loved noting when a ghost appeared, especially in his conversations and personal correspondence. In one typical letter, dated August 5, 1972, he wrote: "The ghosts have been obliging visitors in recent months. The Crying Baby has been heard again, most distinctly." And, he continued, an English visitor encountered the "Man in the Checked Coat and High Collar." Kirk assumed it was his great uncle, Raymond, who had died because a crazy person had beat his head in with a hammer. Interestingly enough, the recipient of this letter was long-time friend Ray Bradbury. When Piety Hill burned to the ground in 1975, many witnesses claimed ghostly apparitions departed the structure through the burning windows. Pictures of the event do indeed reveal strange shapes and faces—many of which vaguely resemble Kirk's long-dead relatives—fleeing.

Logically, if initially counter-intuitively, Kirk's writing of ghost stories makes sense with his own understanding of conservatism as a protection, cultivation, and advancement of timeless truths. Just as Kirk believed human existence to form a continuity from Adam to the last man—through the Logos—so too did a continuity exist from the lowest being to the perfection of the Holy Trinity in the great chain of being. A ghost, as Kirk understood it, was a soul trapped between physical and eternal existence. More often than not, they deserve our pity or appreciation rather than our anger or disgust or fear. Towards those who haunted his house, Kirk felt only wonder and admiration. Somehow, they connected him to time, family, hearth, and home. They haunted him.

> The continuity of family, building, and even furniture in my Mecosta house presumably favors the faithful survival of traces of a vanished consciousness, and reminds one of Santayana's theory that emotion may imbed itself in matter, to be detached long after by another consciousness under peculiar conditions of receptivity. I have no desire to exorcise. If shades tolerate me, I tolerate them.[3]

It's also worth remembering the obvious—that a haunting comes from beyond time, but somehow mysteriously ties the present to the past. A Catholic shrine, a place of pilgrimage, is as haunted as is a house that experienced a brutal murder.

Kirk and Stephen King have a great deal in common, especially in a desire to entertain by openly professing a belief in something much larger than observable and quantifiable reality. Certainly, King is fundamentally more sensationalistic and willing to employ gratuitous language and noxiously graphic sex scenes in a way Kirk would never have even considered. Kirk, instead, allows one to realize what is happening in the background without the need to be explicit. "She cursed Yolande foully and at length," Kirk writes in his short story "The Princess of All Lands." The reader knows that such R-rated events occur, but she or he does not need the author to make it blatant. One can only contemplate what King might do with such a scene. Instead of a seven-word sentence which tells the reader all he or she needs to know, King would write a page or two, describing every minute aspect of the conversation with the foulest language possible made explicit. The important exception in King's

---

3. RAK also believed the High Street, the street upon which sat his Pittenweem, Scotland, house in the 1960s and 1970s, to be haunted. Supposedly, a hanged gypsy from 1888 still prowled the area. When traveling, RAK often sought out the ghostly. In 1967, for example, he visited the Thomas Whaley house in San Diego. "This venerable residence (which has a courtroom in its wings) positively overflows with ghosts," he claimed.

writing is his profound, meaningful, and terrifying second novel, *Salem's Lot*. The story of Stoker's Dracula, set in Maine in 1975 and 1976, it ably explores the nature of sin and heroism, leaving behind King's overuse of the foul and unremittingly dark and employing perhaps the best style of his long career. Perhaps not surprisingly, Kirk and King also shared a literary agent, Kirby McCauley. Equally unsurprisingly, King considered a collection of his short stories, *Princess of All Lands*, one of the finest hundred books of our era.

While King possesses a darker imagination and a distaste for all organized religion—what he once called "Dark Christianity"—the difference between the two authors is a matter of degree. As Jim Person points out, Kirk's memoir of the horrors of Mecosta County, "Lost Lake"—fictionalized in his "Off the Sand Road"—offers a reality of evil far beyond anything King ever conceived. In "Lost Lake," Kirk tells the story of several children playing a game with the body of a dead baby.

> Some months later, the Van Tassell children invited some classmates home to play with their new doll. This was in the dead of winter. When the guests arrived, they did indeed find the Van Tassel children sliding downhill on a sled with a new doll. But that new doll was a human baby, the youngest Van Tassel, dead and frozen stiff. The baby had died the previous week, and had been put into the woodshed for burial when the frost was out of the ground; the other children had asked if they might have the corpse for a doll, and Mrs. Van Tassel had given it to them.

The two authors even appeared together in several collections, and in their non-fiction, the two possess a remarkably similar writing style. They also each possess a love for the wonder of children, a distrust of authorities as well as materialism, a skepticism about the latent cultural Calvinism of New England, a distaste for urban renewal, and a desire to explore questions of free will and predestination. Perhaps most strikingly in hindsight, each could be considered a regional writer. Whereas Kirk explored central Michigan, King's best works consider the quirks of western Maine. King's fictional Maine towns of Castle Rock, Jerusalem's Lot, and Derry seem barely to cover the abyss, allowing the most evil of things to enter into this world, generation after generation. Kirk offers a similar idea in his own Michigan fiction, calling Mecosta County "Potawat-tomie County" and Mecosta village "Bear City." In an important non-fiction essay, though often included in Kirk's fiction, "Lost Lake," the Michiganian describes the power of place and the linger-ing evil it might contain. Around Lost Lake in particular, though in Mecosta County in general, "the genius loci is malevolent," he argued. Barely evolved past tundra, "the land is blown-sand with a precarious inch or two of humus deposited upon it." But Lost Lake was even more evil than Mecosta County. Even the local wildlife has enough sense to ignore the area of Lost Lake, he continued. The weather operated strangely there as well. "A fatality clings to some places," he continued, "not merely to historic houses and battle-fields, but to obscure corners recorded only in the short and simple annals of the poor." Kirk makes a similar point about the area west of St. Andrew's, Scotland. Perhaps in the way that saints and martyrs make a ground holy, allowing it to reflect the Edenic elements of pre-fallen creation and the light of the Logos, certain areas cannot escape the dreadful effects of the fall. King and Kirk are not alone among American authors to make such a claim. Willa Cather's very disturbing chapter "Snake Root" in *Death Comes for the Archbishop* (1927) offers the antediluvian voices of the damned who had for centuries received the offerings of living babies. One can also find similar arguments made explicitly and sometimes merely lingering latently in the works of Nathaniel Hawthorne (New England) and Flannery O'Connor and Walker Percy (both in the American South). Each of these authors employs the idea of an anti-sacramen-tal land, a nexus between living and the abyss. Or, as one of Stephen King's most interesting characters, a father, puts it in the profound and profoundly disturbing novel *It*, "It's because of that soil. . . . It seems that bad things, hurtful things, do right well in the soil of this town. I've thought so again and again over the years. I don't know why it should be . . . but it is." It would be difficult to find a passage in modern horror that more closely resembles Kirk's thoughts on Lost Lake.

In large, however, Kirk's own statement about why he wrote such stories seems correct. "Why did I write these sepulchral fantasies?" he asked. "Why, partly to remind you and myself that we are spirits in prison; and mainly in the hope of discomforting an old man on a winter's night, or a girl in the bloom of her youth." Any work dealing with Kirk that compartmentalizes or dismisses Kirk's storytelling side would not to justice to the man who wrote *The Conservative Mind*. Each aspect is a fundamental aspect of the man. They are aspects not in tension with one another, but in harmony.

Stephen King's Maine

Place matters.

Ever since God exiled Eve and Adam from paradise, we have longed to know place. Sometimes that place is where we are born, sometimes where we will go, and sometimes merely in our brightest (or darkest) imaginings. Most of us—especially in modernity—rarely stay in any once place for too long. We are as restless as we are desirous of surety.

In twentieth-century literature, no one understood this better than Willa Cather. In every one of her stories, she asks repeatedly if we know our place. In his own fiction, the great humanist Russell Kirk also repeatedly asked about the notion of place as understood in geographical space as well as in a Platonic understanding of story.

What we often don't recognize is that our desire to find place is as mythical (Eden) as it is natural. As to the latter point, we would do well to remember the ancient definition of justice: to give each his due. This is, of course, a rather philosophical way of understanding where our place is in society.

For Cather and Kirk, it is worth noting, we can easily misjudge what we believe to be our right place. And we must also recognize that while a place might be holy, it is just as possible for it to be unholy, especially if abuses have been committed over and over again on the same soil. Such a place becomes "haunted," so to speak, radiating the abyss of hell rather than grace of God.

For Cather, these places are almost always redeemable. The grave of a suicide, for example, might become a crossroads, a spot that all revere, even though the reasons why have disappeared with the passage of time.

Kirk, however, remained more skeptical. In both his fiction and non-fiction, he argued that the rape of Michigan's forests might forever make a certain soil more hospitable to evil than to good. Such, he thought, was the case for his own Mecosta County. The "genius loci is malevolent," he wrote of his county, as noted previously in this book. Despair lingered over his home soil, he feared. Indeed,

Kirk seems to have considered himself, his ancestral home, and his family almost as sentinels of good, keeping watch on the growing evil around each. Kirk was, it seems, a sort of American Heimdahl.

Cather and Kirk have long since passed out of time, but one of their most important followers, Stephen King, writes stunningly of place, whether in Maine, Nebraska, or Colorado.

Since sometime in my later junior high years, I've been rather in love with Maine. Granted, I've only been to the actual state three times in my life. Yet I have visited it too many times to count—at least in my deepest imaginings. My love for that most northern of New England states came exclusively from the realm of imagination and imaginative literature. Back in the earliest years of the 1980s, Stephen King's fiction made Maine seem as mysterious as it was magical, full of horror and heroism, a place located in this world but not necessarily in this time frame. A third of a century later, King's Maine still intrigues me almost as much as Tolkien's Middle-earth and Bradbury's Mars.

Many of King's stories take place not just in Maine, but in three Maine towns: Castle Rock, Salem's Lot, and Derry. Feel free to look for them the next time you visit that most northeastern of states. Sadly, no matter how much you look, you will never find any of these towns in any official road atlas or on Google Earth.

These three towns exist (well, to varying degrees, as evil has taken its toll on each) strictly in the heart and soul of Stephen King and in those of his readers. There is no place in Maine actually called Castle Rock, Salem's Lot, or Derry.

Using artificial geographies, though, we can somewhat determine where each would exist were Stephen King's mind completely accurate in matters of this reality.

King's Castle Rock would exist somewhere southwest of Rumford, 20 or so miles from the New Hampshire border. Of his stories, the most important that are placed there are *Dead Zone, Cujo, The Dark Half, Needful Things*, and the short story "The Body" (the basis for the movie *Stand by Me*).

One-hundred-twenty miles to the east of Castle Rock is another King place of fictional wonder, Derry, Maine, home to another whole set of his stories, including the spectacular *It*. This town, as King has described, sits just west of the very real town of Bangor.

If one headed northeast from Castle Rock and northwest from Derry, he would find Salem's Lot, home to the novel of the same name. This is the hardest of towns to pinpoint on the map, but it appears to exist southwest of the real Maine town of Chesuncook.

The three seem to form a kind of "Bermuda Triangle" in which anything can happen, and women, men, and children as well as towns frequently succumb to the darkness of the abyss and disappear from all realities. As the father of a main character in *It* tries to explain to his son, "It's because of that soil. It seems that bad things, hurtful things, do right well in the soil of this town. I've thought so again and again over the years. I don't know why it should be . . . but it is."

In Stephen King's Maine, temptations linger and sins multiply in this triangle of the absurd, but nobility exists as well. Indeed, it would be difficult to find a modern writer in any genre who understands and explores the notions of place better than does King.

And yet, one might complain, King is "just" a horror writer. True. But, who better to understand the evils that plague us?

Salem's Lot

On November 17, 1979, two months after I had turned twelve, I stupidly sneaked out of my bedroom and quietly crept down the stairs. From that vantage point, I watched a bit of Stephen King's *Salem's Lot*, a CBS made-for-TV movie that was the talk of seemingly everyone leading up to that night. Understandably and quite properly, my mom had forbidden me to watch it. Filled with certainty that I was way too old to be scared, I watched it, though covertly.

And though I did not get caught by my mother that night, I certainly received my punishment. For years—far into adulthood—the images that I saw that night on the TV have haunted my imagination… and not haunted in the good way. In particular, I can see in my mind's eye two vampiric figures arising in a basement, their eyes glowing and their would-be victim completely unaware of the danger. The face of each figure was rather featureless, making them even more terrifying in their lack of distinctive will and personality.

A few years later, around age fourteen, I started reading the actual fiction of Stephen King, and I rather fell in love with it. I avoided *Salem's Lot*, however, as it had simply terrified me too much as a kid.

Finally, as an adult, I decided the best way to exorcise these lingering memories was to read the book. I did. And I was more than impressed. Prior to reading *Salem's Lot*, I would happily have labeled Mr. King a first-rate storyteller but not a top-notch writer. The man can produce incredibly complicated plots, and many of his characters are so well-sketched-out as to seem real to me. Mr. King is especially good when describing the imagination of a child and the child's ability to see things the adult no longer can. Additionally, Mr. King can write about the righteousness of a child better than any other contemporary writer.

My disappointment with Mr. King, however, comes in his lingering over evil. For example, rather than explaining that someone was murdered, it generally takes him four or five pages to drag the reader through the actual letting of blood and the spilling of guts. Too much at times.

Though equally dark in tone in his own fiction, for example, Russell Kirk would explain that a murder had occurred, but leave the vast possibilities of that murder—in its details and specifics—to the imagination of the reader. In a sense, Kirk's approach allows one to experience an even more terrifying scene, as the murder becomes intimately real to the reader rather than merely an almost journalistic and factual blow-by-blow of myriad details.

My view of Mr. King's writing, however, changed dramatically the first time I finally read *Salem's Lot*. The writing style was, to my surprise, not just good, but excellent. In part, he artistically avoided the foul language and gore so readily employed in his later fiction. In so doing, he made the novel not only better as art, but scarier as a story.

Salem's Lot is, rather blatantly, a re-write of Bram Stoker's *Dracula*, but set in a modern (1975) setting. A young widowed writer returns to his boyhood home in Jerusalem's Lot, Maine. Haunted by childhood memories of having explored the tortured Marsden mansion that overlooks the town, Ben Mears seeks to exorcise his own demons by immersing himself in the lore of the town and the home. Very quickly, he realizes that an evil pervades all, especially after a dog is brutally murdered and several children disappear. Together with his plucky girlfriend, the high school English teacher, a brilliant pre-teen boy (Mark), a local physician, and the parish priest, Mears combats the evil that has recently arrived from Europe and planted itself in the town.

Over the last generation, vampires have become so pervasive in Hollywood culture as to become ineffectual as scary creatures. Vampires as traditionally understood, though, should be horrifying images of what the human person is not. Not alive and not dead, they walk the earth as parasites, controlled only by their insatiable yearnings for human life and blood and by those who tempted them or consumed them into a non-life. They cannot exist in sunlight, and they can do nothing unless so invited. In other words, they embody the perfect anti-man. Not surprisingly, in nineteenth-century Protestant literature, authors often presented Catholics priests as vampiric, preying on the unsuspecting women of their parishes. Frankly, this is a compliment to the Church, as it reveals just how frightening a bad priest can be as opposed to the true goodness of a holy one.

Though certainly not Catholic, Stephen King realizes the only solution to fighting the vampires in his novel comes from the Catholic Church.

As mentioned above, though, it is the writing style that Mr. King employs in this novel that appeals to the discerning reader. Below is a sample of not only the excellent writing style, but the invocation of childhood heroism that so distinguishes Mr. King from other current novelists.

> Before drifting away entirely, he found himself reflecting—not for the first time—on the peculiarity of adults. They took laxatives, liquor, or sleeping pills to drive away their terrors so that sleep would come, and their terrors were so tame and domestic: the job, the money, what the teacher will think if I can't get Jennie nicer clothes, does my wife still love me, who are my friends. They were pallid compared to the fears every child lies cheek and jowl with in his dark bed, with no one to confess to in hope of perfect understanding but another child. There is no group therapy or psychiatry or community social services for the child who must cope with the thing under the bed or in the cellar every night, the thing which leers and capers and threatens just beyond the point where vision will reach. The same lonely battle must be fought night after night and the only cure is the eventual ossification of the imaginary faculties, and this is called adulthood. . . . Tonight Mark Petrie had faced one [a real terror; a vampire], and ten minutes later lay in the lap of sleep, the plastic cross still grasped loosely in his right hand like a child's rattle. Such is the difference between men and boys. (King, *Salem's Lot*, 372–73)

Is there a natural connection of conservatism and of horror fiction with movies? If one can effectively separate what is slasher from what is horror, then horror becomes not merely a good genre, but a brilliant one. It allows us to confront the horrors of this world in symbolic terms, thus giving us distance and, paradoxically, objectivity. Just as Halloween mocks the Enemy, so, too, does horror when probably exercised.

V for Vendetta

Throw together an English Roman Catholic terrorist from 1605; a 1930s noir atmosphere; a damsel who is only somewhat in distress; a government that makes Orwell's Ingsoc look humane; some psyche-delics; some fortuitous but random evangelical proof-texting of *The Collected Works of William Shakespeare*; some references to the mass killings of the twentieth century; a bit of Ray Bradbury, Max Ernst, and Patrick McGoohan; a rather tame lesbian romance; some raging pagan will power; a fictional 1980s that went exactly against what actually happened; some inspiration from William Butler Yeats and "anarchy loosed upon the world"; and two young cocksure, perfec-tionist English artists who want to avoid mimicking their American counterparts. You probably still would not end up with the disturb-ing masterpiece that is *V for Vendetta*.

Written in the first third of the 1980s but not published as a graphic novel until 1988, *V for Vendetta* broke into the cultural mindset of the rising intellectual generation like nothing else.

For someone coming of age in that decade—with New Wave, *Blade Runner*, Ronald Reagan, *The Day After*, Rush, Macintosh, Red Rain, and Nuclear Winter—*V for Vendetta* took the extreme desires and fears of a whole generation and made them into a coherent (mostly) tale.

If John Hughes captured our most adolescent suburban libertine longings, *V for Vendetta* re-made them into our most terrifying lib-ertarian nightmare.

England Prevails

The story, written by Alan Moore and David Lloyd, takes place in the late 1990s. In 1983, a British Labour government replaced the Tories, kicking out the American nuclear missiles, and thus leaving the U.K. free from atomic destruction. Soon, the Americans and the Soviets went after each other, desolating America.

The resulting economic turmoil in Europe led to the rise of a National Socialist/fascist government in Britain. Though the leaders personally gave into every perverse and lewd pleasure, in and out of their bedrooms, they outlawed homosexuality, non-whites, and non-Protestant Christians. Imagine Cromwell morphing into a hyperweaponized Jim Bakker, and you come close to the "Dear Leader" of fascist Britain.

Those who were neither deported nor executed found themselves in prison camps, the playthings of progressive eugenicists, willing to see the body contorted and deconstructed in every possible manner to "perfect the race."

Under the slogan "England Prevails," the fascists maintain control through mass surveillance as well as through armed thugs known as "Finger Men" who have the power to kill, rape, and pillage at will, all in the name of England. Signs litter the streets with the hypocritical propaganda: "Strength through Purity; Purity through Faith." Superficial TV programming—such as the story of "Storm Saxon," a thinly veiled Mike Hammer character, full of white racial pride, fighting back African invaders in the year 2501—keep the masses entertained and distracted from food shortages and poor health care. "Die you black cannibal filth! Die! Die! Die!" he screams, as he opens fire upon some non-Anglo Saxons.

Of the internment camps, one of the most brutal was the Larkhill Settlement, out of which emerged the anarchist anti-hero, V. The authors intentionally keep his identity hidden, as he represents an idea more than a person. Toward the end of the novel, when confronted by a government agent, V explains, "There. Did you think to kill me? There's no flesh or blood within this cloak to kill. There's only an idea. Ideas are bullet proof."

Still, the reader does come to know that V had been interned and had survived the experiments. In some way, never explained, the experiments made him more human than human, endowing him with extraordinary powers of resistance to bodily harm, astounding concentration and memory, and near-perfect agility. It would, however, be better to describe the final product of the experiment as the creation of a Batman rather than a Superman. The only one of the test subjects to live, V, gained the favor of his captors, set the camp aflame, and escaped.

Poetic Assassinations

The main story takes place years after the destruction of Larkhill. Now, one by one, every person who ever worked at Larkhill is being systematically murdered; though the more appropriate term would be "assassinated." V, of course, is proudly the killer. Looking a bit like an early-seventeenth-century Batman, he wears a Guy Fawkes mask, a buckled hat, and a massive cloak, under which he hides an assortment of bladed weapons. V not only kills his victims, but he does so with immense poetic justice. Each person assassinated—reminiscent of Dante's *Inferno*—dies according to his or her vice.

He can temper his killings with mercy, but he kills nonetheless. When confronting Dr. Delia Surridge, once so disgusted by all deviations from the norm but now repentant, V murders her without pain.

> No. No, I thought I would be [afraid], but I'm not. I'm . . . relieved. Oh, God, all these years, all this waiting. You see, I always knew you'd come back. When I saw you that night . . . The night you escaped, you were standing against the flames. You turned and looked straight at me. I knew then that one day you'd come looking for me, that you'd find me. What . . . what we did, what I did at Larkhill. That terrible knowledge. It's been with me so long. That I could do things like that.

In her admission, she recounts a study conducted in America before her fall. Students had volunteered for an experiment to administer shocks to victims when commanded. The victims were actors, but the student volunteers did not know this. They believed themselves to be administering immense pain. "Nearly 80% of those tested carried on administering shocks after the 'victim' begged them to stop. Nearly 60% continued even after they believed that they'd killed him."

Her explanation for such horrors:

> They were ordinary people and they were prepared to torture a stranger to death just because they were told to by someone in authority. Some of them said they'd even enjoyed it. I think I enjoyed what I did at the time. People are stupid and evil. There's

something wrong with us. Some hideous flaw . . . we deserved to be culled.

As she fades peacefully from the world, she asks V to remove his Guy Fawkes mask. "It's beautiful," she ejaculates as she dies.

The entire story of V takes place over a period of a little more than a year, November 5, 1997, to November 1998.

The People Choose

V's philosophy of resistance and rebellion offers a rather coherent if not always enticing complexity. It's difficult for the reader to know just how mad V is. Certainly, he's brilliant, trans-human (as tampered with and modified), and suffers from extreme paranoia as well as OCD. This, of course, does not mean his interpretation of events is wrong, only that it comes from the mind of someone on the brink of total insanity.

During the middle of the story, V gains control of government TV. As he does, he recounts the history of tyranny in the twentieth century.

> And what about the children? It's always the children who suffer, as you're well aware. Poor little mites. What are they to make of it? What are they to make of your bullying, your despair, your cowardice and all your fondly nurtured bigotries? Really, it's not good enough, is it? And it's no good blaming the drop in work standards upon bad management, either . . . though, to be sure, the management is very bad. In fact, let us not mince words. . . . The management is terrible.

During V's soliloquy, images of Hitler, Stalin, and Mussolini flash upon the screen.

> We've had a string of embezzlers, frauds, liars and lunatics making a string of catastrophic decisions. This is plain fact. But who elected them? It was you! You who appointed these people! You who gave them to the power to make your decisions for you! While I'll admit that anyone can make a mistake once, to go on making the same lethal errors century after century seems to me nothing short of deliberate. You have encouraged these malicious incompetents, who have made your working life a shambles. You

have accepted without question their senseless orders. You have allowed them to fill your workspace with dangerous and unproven machines. You could have stopped them. All you had to say was "no."

For Moore and Lloyd, democracy has proven incapable of sustaining the good life. When asked why he would not proceed through the political system, V replies, "It does not do to rely too much on silent majorities, Evey [the female protagonist], for silence is a fragile thing. . . . One loud noise, and it's gone."

Though the story is terribly violent at a personal and societal level, there are moments of sheer beauty. Toward the end of the story, as V knows that he must go into battle openly, he tells Evey, "Persevere, Eve. Understanding music, we may hear the music that there is in life from its first insufficient trills . . . unto its closing minor chords." Whatever the violence, he continues, never forget the pleasure of knowledge, the pleasure of creativity, and the "higher attributes of reason, love and culture."

V for Vendetta is a beautiful if terrifying work of art. Though a graphic novel, it is most certainly NOT for children. In its ability to explain the human person as well as the horrors of Leviathan, it rivals *1984* and *The Handmaid's Tale*.

V?

What is V? Victory? The Roman Numeral 5? Vendetta? Vengeance? Beethoven's Fifth?

The authors never explain. But, with a story of this depth and breadth, we wouldn't want too much thrust into the face. A little mystery is good for all of us.

Far more than a penny for the old Guy.

The High Cost of Virtue: *The Watchmen*

Who watches the watchmen, who guards the guardians?

In the early- to mid-1980s, two very talented if utterly eccentric English men—Alan Moore and Dave Gibbons—produced a masterpiece of fiction, *The Watchmen*.

The form the piece took is almost as fascinating as the story itself. Though Moore claims the medium he helped pioneer is really nothing more than a glorified comic book given a new and clever name by marketers, the "graphic novel" might be properly regarded as the first new medium in books since the mass market paperback appeared on shelves in 1935 in England and in 1939 in America. A cross between a comic book and a coffee-table book, the graphic novel has grown from novelty to mainstream in a mere thirty-plus years of existence. Now, it's impossible to enter a used or new bookstore without a section (often quite extensive) dedicated to the graphic novel. A number of academic examinations of the graphic novel as a specific medium exist as well, but I have yet to find one that is not full of ridiculous deconstructionist language, full of "queer" or "gendered" points. I almost wrote "ideas" instead of "points" in this previous sentence, but "ideas" is simply too solid and too kind a word to allow it to be associated with the nonsense that passes as literary theory these days—which, of course, is nothing but a scam.

Though several books produced in the 1970s might be regarded as "graphic novels" in hindsight, they were merely a collection of various stories under one cover. The four that caught the attention of the public and the critics, all published in the mid-1980s, were *The Watchmen*, *V for Vendetta* (also by Moore), *The Dark Knight Returns* by Frank Miller, and *Maus* by Art Spiegelman. Others that have sold well over the past several decades or have been critically acclaimed: *Rising Stars* and *Midnight Nation* by J. Michael Straczynski; *Ronin* by Frank Miller; *DMZ* by Brian Wood; *Grendel* by Matt Wagner; *The Last Man* by Brian K. Vaughan; and *Identity Crisis* by Brad Meltzer.

Whatever its origins, the graphic novel has certainly become a distinctive medium over the last three decades, whether a glorified comic book or not. Two things can be stated rather definitely about the form. First, it really is neither book nor movie. Instead, it might be regarded as a well-expressed, well-developed, and finely honed type of script and storyboarding directors use when making movies.

Second, a graphic novel probably has more in common with stained glass than any book produced since the Gutenberg Bible. One would not be radically off to claim it as a mythological and pre-Reformation art form, though it is utterly modern. For all intents and purposes, a graphic novel is stained glass in motion, a manuscript not just illuminated but also animated.

Though I have given a lot of thought to the art form, I certainly do not want to present myself as an expert. I have, however, had the privilege of teaching the graphic novel as an art form to a number of students—at Hillsdale as well as at CU-Boulder—and the medium never ceases to fascinate them, especially when some of the symbolism becomes obvious. And, frankly, the medium fascinates me as well, as I assume is obvious from the above. I like to think of the graphic novel as a means by which word and image can become one again, a sort of sacramental pop culture.

* * *

Israel's watchmen are blind, they all lack knowledge; they are all mute dogs, they cannot bark; they lie around and dream, they love to sleep. They are dogs with mighty appetites; they never have enough. They are shepherds who lack understanding; they all turn to their own way, each seeks his own gain.—Isaiah 56:10–12

Sed quis custodiet ipsos custodes?—Juvenal, *Satire* 6

The story of *The Watchmen* takes place in an alternative or parallel 1985, a world deeply cynical, a world that found no solace after Nixon. Actually, somehow, in 1985, Richard Nixon is still the president of the United States. The Cold War has become so intense that the clock of Atomic Scientists is only moments before midnight, an all-out nuclear war looms over the entire world. Where there had been a golden age of superheroes (akin to the all-American Superman), many of their followers had become less than virtuous. And, it turns out, not all that seemed to glitter in the first era of superheroes had been gold. Moore and Gibbons deal frankly with societal decay, with paranoia, with justice, with injustice, with child abuse, and with the role of conformity in society. Philosopher Aeon Skoble has written the single finest essay on *The Watchmen* as graphic novel. Skoble sees the story as being as much about real world events as it is about "the psychology as well as the ethical and political ramifications of vigilantism." In other words, what is a man (or woman) to do, when the government corrupts rather than protects. When does it become not just a right to defend oneself against injustice but an actual moral and ethical duty to do so?

To avoid the reactions one would expect from their legion of fans by making Superman, Batman, or Wonder Woman less than heroic in their graphic novel, Moore and Gibbons wisely chose to remake a set of superheroes and their self-contained universe originally created by Charlton Comics (1944–1983) but, as of 1985, owned but rarely used by DC. In *The Watchmen*, the "superheroes" are Nite Owl (the closest to Batman); Dr. Manhattan (the closest to Superman); The Comedian (imagine a Soldier of Fortune-Joker); Ozymandias (think a hyper-intelligent Steve Jobs on steroids); Silk Spectre (a highly sexualized 1940s version of Wonder Woman); and, by far the most interesting, Rorschach, a paranoid genius and unrelenting vigilante who refuses to turn himself over to the U.S. government.

Moore and Gibbons have created something so far removed from the stereotype of comics for kids that many of the scenes—so realistically told and drawn—shock even those of us who have become a little too jaded in this modern world. One of the most stunning (and horrific) moments in the book is when the "heroes" begin to let loose against the North Vietnamese. The brutality encouraged and allowed by the U.S. government against civilians is matched only in modern cultural manifestations by such movies as *Apocalypse Now* and *Platoon*.

Quotes from everything in western culture from the Old Testament to William Blake to Bob Dylan litter the book, each more relevant than the last. And the two creators of *The Watchmen* give not only an extensive background to their alternative 1985 but insights of the characters themselves. Indeed, the development of the characters in *The Watchmen* is as good as if not far better than any modern novel by the John Updikes or the John Irvings of the world.

> The streets are extended gutters and the gutters are full of blood and when the drains finally scab over, all the vermin will drown. The accumulated filth of all their sex and murder will foam up about their waists and all the whores and politicians will look up and shout "save us"... and I'll look down and whisper "no."—Rorschach's Journal, October 12, 1985.

As mentioned above, the character of Rorschach (AKA Walter Kovacs) is by far the most fascinating. He is relentless in his pursuit of real justice, and he alone—however brutally—maintains the ideals of righteous vengeance that the other heroes have given up, pursing normal life, marketing stardom, godhood, and even simple sloth. He must do whatever he can, even at the risk of exposing himself to law enforcement, to keep the various desires and pursuits of the heroes in check and honed for doing good. Not only is Rorschach brutal physically, he's also brutal in his politically incorrect views of the world.

The story of *The Watchmen* is so powerful because it is not a story of good vs. evil but a story of good vs. apathy, a story of being vs. annihilation. It deals not with the superficial but with the things that matter most in this world. It is a story of failures, successes, tragedies, and the human condition. It never shies away from controversy, and it never takes the easy route.

As the world moves closer and closer to its end, the heroes must re-find and re-claim their daring virtue. It's not easy, and, to make matters worse, someone is trying to murder them, one by one.

After years of discussions and false starts, Zack Snyder, one of our greatest living film directors and a man of unsurpassed cinematic genius, bravely made a movie version of the graphic novel. If you've been fortunate enough to watch Snyder's *300*, *Man of Steel*, or *Batman v. Superman*, you know this is a creator who never does anything halfway. He also loves spectacle, and he's unafraid to show the necessary and very high price for true heroism. When *The Watchmen* first came out, critics lambasted it, but even in the adulterated form that the studio forced upon the theatrical release (the studio being fearful audiences could not handle three hours' worth of the movie), genius sneaks through rather visibly at times.

In its theatrical form, the movie is 162 minutes. In its "ultimate form," the movie is 218 minutes. Those extra 56 minutes make all the difference in the world, and things that might seem confusing to the average movie-goer seem full and deep in the ultimate version.

However you want to take in *The Watchmen*—graphic novel or ultimate cut of the movie—it's well worth your time. In a world of horrors abroad and vanilla conformism and acceptable corruption at home, *The Watchmen* gleefully tears off the scab, revealing modernity in all of its ugliness and dripping puss. But it also demonstrates that greatness—true greatness the Roman republicans would have admired—still exists, but the cost to reclaim it is certainly high.

The Audacity of Frank Miller

Frank Miller raged.
He stood naked at the edge of the skyscraper. The streets lay far below him. A frozen explosion of steel and glass burst in flight to the sky over the motionless traffic. The traffic seemed immovable, the steel and glass flowing. The steel and glass had the stillness of one brief moment in battle when thrust meets thrust and the currents are held in a pause more dynamic than motion. The steel and glass glowed, wet with sunrays. (With apologies to Miss Rand and the writers of the Christian Gospels)

There is no doubting that the attack on the World Trade Centers on September 11, 2001, fundamentally shaped one of the greatest and most innovative artists of the last half-century, Frank Miller.

Though his name might not be instantly recognizable to many readers, his shadow hangs over much of popular culture. Films, novels, and television shows—directly and indirectly—reveal daily his vast imprint on American culture. While many book sellers and critics do not consider graphic novels serious literature, his 1986 work *The Dark Knight Returns* has sold over three million copies, making it a continuous best seller since its initial publication. Even Miller himself despises the term "graphic novel," believing it sounds too much like something risqué. Still, there's no denying its success and importance. Miller believes that writers, artists, and readers should embrace the "graphic novel" for what it is: a comic book, plain and simple.

Frank Miller is to comics and film what Neil Peart was to rock and what Camille Paglia is to academia. He is nothing less than himself. Always and everywhere, he is purely Frank Miller. It seems he could be nothing other than Frank Miller. If he changes, he can only become even more Frank Miller. On September 11, 2001, Frank Miller became more fully Frank Miller.

Those of us not on the political and cultural Left should celebrate him as a radical and unreconstructed individualist, the kind that only North America seems capable of producing in the post-modern world, a man never afraid to voice his views, whether commensurate with the bullying and mindless nightmares of the mob or not.

The Emerging Talent

Born in 1957 to Irish-American Roman Catholics, Miller grew up in Vermont, one of seven children. From about age five, he fell head over heels in love with comics, and his parents encouraged and nurtured this passion. At times, he found his early adult careers on the edge of derailment. Finishing high school because of the advice of his parents, Miller tried his hand at janitorial work, at transporting goods in trucking, and at driving buses. Every boss he had prior to entering the field of comics fired him.

In the late 1970s, as he lost job after job, he began to study with the then-best artist in the comic world, Neal Adams. After working at Gold Key comics and on lesser-known titles at DC, Miller moved to Marvel and soon took over the then nearly defunct character Daredevil. Much to the surprise of all at Marvel and in the comic world, Miller wrote what is now considered the definitive Daredevil, an anguished and blind Matt Murdock who regularly seeks the sacrament of Confession, confiding in his parish priest, as he wonders just how far he can fight in the name of vigilante justice. With Miller as writer, Daredevil went from relative obscurity to being one of Marvel's finest, most nuanced, and most popular comics. After working on his independent cyberpunk comic and hero for DC, Ronin, Miller then moved to Batman. Miller not only revived the then-failing character but, along with Alan Moore and his *Watchman*, also revitalizing the entire comic industry, then on the edge of bankruptcy.

An avowed gnostic, a Leftist, and a seemingly particular person, Alan Moore soon left the industry in boredom and disgust, but Miller stuck with it. A monumentally determined perfectionist, Miller kept his politics much closer to his chest than had Moore, though his quietly expressed views almost always embraced a kind of Goldwater libertarianism. Trying to improve his writing, Miller also read and studied like mad. He read everything from Dashiell Hammett to Robert Heinlein to Christopher Lasch, and he studied Japanese and European comic styles. Restless and curious to the nth degree, he became an amateur anthropologist as he traveled throughout Asia and the Near East, observing everything from cultural norms to speech patterns to the shades of light hitting the landscape. His reading and traveling, combined with his love of cinema, seeing everything from Hitchcock to *Dirty Harry*, honed his art—in drawing and writing—to create modern myth, centering around the hero and anti-hero, around good and evil, and around beauty and chaos.

If understood properly, Miller persuasively argued, heroes bring us back to first principles of "right and wrong." "I love heroes, I believe in heroism. I also adore fantasy, and so I'm drawn back to these superheroes," Miller explained in October 2016. "Their mythology is open to infinite expansion, and the basic myth is irresistible. They got so much right in that first Superman movie, down to the tagline 'you'll believe a man can fly.' That's our job."

His explicit goal has always been "to do heroic adventures without compromise." Too much of modern culture, he complains in the vein of Russell Kirk and C. Wright Mills, has become nothing but conformist drivel, with movies, television shows, and comic books serving the public as heavy "sedatives." Instead, we need the Batmans and Dirty Harrys to bring the "wrath of God" down upon the murderers, rapists, and tyrants of the world. The world desperately needs morality, order, and myth.

With his trademark fedora, open jacket, t-shirt, and scruffy white beard, Miller might look almost as unpleasant as Alan Moore really is. But watch an interview with Miller and you'll find he's about the nicest guy in the world.

Unforgivable

On the tenth anniversary of 9/11, Miller did something unforgivable to the politically correct mafia as well as to the state of Iran (which condemned him, he proudly reminds us). He published a graphic novel, *Holy Terror*, in which the bad guys are Islamic fundamentalists. The first release of the then-fledgling company Legendary Comics, a subsidiary of Legendary Pictures, *Holy Terror* horrified most of the media, formal and social. In the press release that launched the book, though, Miller's editor, Bob Schreck, wrote: "It has been my extreme pleasure and honor to have worked so closely with Frank for over 20 years now." The new graphic novel "finds Frank at the top of his game. A fast-paced, biting commentary on our uncertain and volatile times, told with some of the most gut-wrenching, iconic images he's ever produced."

Schreck, though, stood affront a tidal wave of epic proportions. *Wired* called it "one of the most appalling, offensive, and vindictive comics of all time," a product of "9/11 decadence," a "horror" of America's "carefully nurtured grievance." *ThinkProgress* claimed Miller was "viciously Islamophobic" and took pleasure in the "sexualization of torture." Others called it a "mean and ugly book," "sickening," a book about "rage-aholics with a limited vocabulary," "fodder for the Anti-Islam set," a "revenge fantasy" of a person who has removed himself "from reality," and "sloppy, arrogant work by an arrogant bastard." Even Miller's hero and mentor, Neal Adams, claimed (without details of how and where) that Miller had allowed his work to consume him, claiming Miller had become "white trash."

In the year following the book's publication, Miller unapologetically defended *Holy Terror*, explaining, rather rationally, "I lived through a time when 3,000 of my neighbors were incinerated for no apparent reason. I lived through the chalky, smoky weeks that followed and through the warplanes flying overhead and realized that, much like my character, The Fixer, I found a mission." Drawing inspiration from the anti-Nazi and anti-Japanese Empire war comics of the 1940s, Miller saw his own work as the equivalent in the war against terror. No doubt, he openly admitted, "I come in with my own very pro-Western-they-attacked-my-city-point of view." In no way, he continued, did he mean "to be fair or balanced." Interestingly to be sure, Miller had earlier in his career complained that too much in comics was propaganda, not art. "My one attempt at" propaganda, he conceded in the early 1980s, "was a dismal failure." Asked why, he responded, "It was too preachy." A quarter of a century later, though, he was ready to try his hand at it again.

When asked by the London *Guardian* if he would still defend his views as vented through 2011's *Holy Terror*, Miller admitted that the work was, at times, "bloodthirsty beyond belief." Still, he noted, he would never go "back and start erasing books." The *Guardian* took this as an apology, and many in the comic industry and media have since forgiven him.

What was so patently obvious to anyone who knew Frank Miller's work, however, was that *Holy Terror* was no more and no less anti-fundamentalist than his other works. His masterpiece, *The Dark Knight Returns* (1986), attacked Protestant fundamentalism, and his noir series, *Sin City* (1991–), showed the heinous results of Roman Catholic fundamentalism. His recreation of the Battle of Thermopylae, *300*, portrayed the Persians as slavish fundamentalists worshipping a god-king. Though Iran condemned Miller for *300*, most critics gave him a pass (and often high praise) for his anti-Evangelical and anti-Catholic fundamentalism. For a billion reasons, though, they found his anti-Islamic fundamentalism unacceptable. Hypocrites all.

God bless you, Frank Miller

As soon as Miller became secure and successful in the field of comics by the mid 1980s, he not only nurtured anyone who asked for his help, but he also launched a major public campaign for comic companies to better pay their writers and artists upfront as well as in royalties earned. Not only did Miller help resurrect the dying industry, but his example and efforts have since led to a flourishing of talents in and around comics and movies.

Combatting the Jerry Falwell and Tipper Gore busybodies of the 1980s, Miller also attacked censorship at every political level, convincingly arguing that with few exceptions, censors never know what they are doing, while their motives are less than pure. They seek power over society as well as governmental and corporate control over family. Time and again, Miller stressed, it is the sole prerogative of the mother and father to censor material for the family, not the job of the state to do so.

Sometimes, Miller takes his mischievousness to untoward levels of poor taste, such as when he plasters the "Approved by the Comics Code Authority" stamp on a sexy, female robot tart in his stories of Lance Blastoff. Generally, though, the humor is more "junior high level" than it is clever satire. Still, there's a definite humor to it, even when he shocks simply to shock.

While it's tempting to love Miller for the enemies he has made—here in the United States and in Iran—it's far better to praise him for his virtues and his innumerable creations. Through *Daredevil*, he taught us wisdom; through *Batman*, he taught us morality; through *300*, he taught us fortitude; through *Sin City*, he taught us struggle; and through *Martha Washington*, he taught us patriotism. When talking about his own work and its expressions of heroism, he wisely noted that "doing the right thing routinely causes one great difficulties and one has to sacrifice a lot." This is true not just for his heroes, but for Miller himself.

God bless you, Frank.

The Hypergraphia of Kevin J. Anderson

When I found out I was being granted the immense privilege of spending a year at the University of Colorado-Boulder, I knew immediately that one of the most important goals for my year was to meet the husband-wife science-fiction team of Kevin J. Anderson and Rebecca Moesta. Not that I wanted to be a stalker or a troll... I just thought: I will offer an invitation to make contact and see what happens. Much to my delight, Kevin graciously responded to my invitation within hours. Now we have met several times, and I have gained immeasurably from our budding friendship.

I started reading the works of Kevin J. Anderson roughly a quarter-century ago. I wish I could pinpoint the date, but I cannot with exactness. Since first discovering his writings, I have watched his career with great interest. As most readers of *The Imaginative Conservative* know, I love to write. I am rather obsessed with it. I have tried my hand at fiction, but it does not come easily—not that I expect good things to come easily. But, being obsessed with writing, I knew that I would probably have to write about writing, rather than creating whole new worlds. Being especially partial to biographies (and, admittedly, following the lead of Joseph Pearce), I have happily gone the biographer route. Regardless, I had encountered the work of Kevin J. Anderson and J. Michael Straczynski at the same time, and I decided to make a study of their careers as writers, in and out of Hollywood and New York publishing. I thought—and still think—they remain the two most talented writers of our generation in terms of sheer storytelling. Each is just a bit older than I am, and I figured twenty-plus years ago that this would be a perfect long-term project. So it has been. Not only has watching these two greats been fascinating, it has also been intelligently entertaining as well.

Reading Kevin J. Anderson humbles me. You see, Mr. Anderson and I both suffer from what is known properly as hypergraphia, a writing disorder. Neither of us can stop writing. My case, at least in a relative fashion, is minor; Mr. Anderson's is extreme and severe. For every word I write, Anderson writes one hundred.

And, no, I do not offer hyperbole in this assessment. Try as I might, I cannot keep up with Mr. Anderson's books, even as a reader. Though he has only been writing since the late 1980s, he has published some 130 novels, fifty of which have been best sellers. The man's imagination never stops. The genres he explores are fairly limitless, as well: space operas, hard science fiction, military science fiction, fantasies, fairy tales, children's fiction, young adult fiction, graphic novels, essays, writing guides, detective, and horror. He creates his own vast universes—as in the brilliant *Terra Incognita* series, the *Saga of the Seven Suns* series, and the *Dark Between the Star* series (a sequel to the *Saga of the Seven Suns*)—and he also plays in the *Star Wars*, *Star Trek*, *Dune*, *Superman*, *Batman*, and *X-Files* universes. He writes comics, movie novelizations, and rock lyrics, as well. When he is not writing his own stuff, he serves as a sort of guru and mentor to a large community of writers, including Canada's Neil Peart (RIP).

But it would be a mistake to limit him to being "just a writer." He and his wife (Rebecca, with whom he often co-writes) run a successful publishing and writing company as well, WordFire Press. Pioneers in e-publishing, Kevin and Rebecca also run a variety of seminars throughout the year on the art of writing and publishing. WordFire is moving rapidly toward defining the market, having recently acquired the rights, for example, to entire corpus of the late Allen Drury.

As to Kevin's professional background, all of which serves his current writing, publishing, and entrepreneurial talents, he graduated with a physics/astronomy degree from the University of Wisconsin, Madison. The Lawrence Livermore National Laboratory hired him as a technical writer. During his many years in California, he not only met and married the love of his life, the truly impressive Rebecca, but he also published his first novel, the delightfully creepy *Resurrection, Inc.* (1988), a story loosely based on Rush's 1984 album *Grace Under Pressure*.

On January 28, 2015, Mr. Anderson and Ms. Moesta visited us at the University of Colorado-Boulder as a part of the Conservative Thought and Policy program. I have no idea what their politics are, but I can state with certainty that each participant that night walked away rather happy and more than satisfied—electrified by grace and imagination. As if he were not talented enough, Kevin also possesses a natural oratorical skill. For well more than an hour he mesmerized the crowd with the story of his hard work, his rise from obscurity, and his continued persistence and innovation in the face of a radically changing market. He did all of this with humor and humility. Indeed, no one in that audience could have left the auditorium without reveling in a sense of wonder. For Kevin does not just explain his sense of wonder, he invites all into a transcendent and all-encompassing sense of wonder.

Raised in Franksville, Wisconsin, Kevin began to read and write from the first moments possible. Indeed, reading and writing went together for him as naturally as breathing comes to the rest of us. His mother, a former Sauerkraut Queen, and his father, a banker, encouraged their son to explore the worlds of literature and ideas. Kevin told about his first introduction to a library, a bookmobile, the Airmont Classics Library, and to his very own typewriter ("a steampunk version of a laptop"). His first "novel," only three pages long, was called "The Injection." In high school, his history professor let him write a short story about the bubonic plague. A Wisconsin paper published his first story, "Memorial."

And the stories continued, riveting the audience. Each story came as well with Mr. Anderson's self-deprecating humor and his perfect sense of timing.

As he described his own life, he compared it to making popcorn… back before microwave popcorn. No person would ever pop one kernel at a time. Instead, we allow the popcorn—in bunches—to pop as heat works upon each kernel: one shoots one direction, another in the other direction. For Anderson, a writer should approach his craft in the same fashion. As with any profession and talent, writing is as much hard work and skill as it is art. It is best to write and let the ideas flow, taking the writer (and, hopefully, the reader) where they fly, collide, miss, and land.

Upon my first reading of Mr. Anderson's works, now more than two and one-half decades ago, I knew I would love the mind and soul behind those words. Upon my actual meeting of the man, I can state with certainty that Kevin Anderson is not only a genius, but also elegant, eccentric, wise, intelligent, generous, gracious, and a builder of a million vital, overlapping communities.

Whether Mr. Anderson is conservative or not, I have no idea. He is, unquestionably, imaginative, and we are blessed to have his talents in this postmodern world of chaos and sorrows. For Kevin Anderson, in every word and every action, calls us back to the most important and most beautiful things.

Apocalyptic Ponderings

Toward the end of the 20th century, closing two thousand years of history since the time of the Incarnate Christ (or close enough), millennium fever struck the western world hard. A fist across the face and a punch to the stomach. Many fundamentalist Christians were calculating the time since Israel's re-creation as a marker, while a number of Catholics were counting down the number of good, true, and legitimate popes remaining before a supposed anti-pope arose. The Virgin Mary had supposedly appeared in former Yugoslavia, dropping hints about popes and anti-popes and a variety of other fancies that many assumed were not fanciful. Radical doomsday cults (well, are there any other kind?) emerged out of the woodwork—or seeped into the aquifers in Yellowstone, depending on what kind of fuel and storage tanks they were using for the End—and evangelical authors had a field day (and a billion runs to the bank) predicting the End in fictional form.

Would you be Left Behind? What kind of Tribulation would there be? And, at what altitude? At the top of the stairwell? Eight stories up? Eight miles high? Would JC rule before the New Jerusalem arrived, or after? Would humans build the City of God here and now? How many seals would be broken by angels? Just who is that fourth horseman? And why are Catholics the only ones worried about that dragon devouring Mary?

Of course, it's not all religious. Remember the fears regarding Y2K. Were you ready? Just how angular could all of this be?

The End is near!!!! The End is near!!!! Very near, dammit!

Sadly, such fever and fervor has yet to subside, really. We were just treated ("subjected" would be a more appropriate word to use) to a remake of the horrific, hate-filled *Left Behind*, this time with Hollywood superstar Nicholas Cage fronting. Why couldn't the dear leader of North Korea have gone after that one instead of the one from Sony? Sheesh, many might have even become convinced he is the anti-Christ. He'd probably like that.

We worried about Harold Camping's two predictions of the end.

Both were wrong. We worried about the Mayans ending their calendar. Nope. Even the Vikings seemed to have predicted the end right around now. Again, didn't happen.

In fact, I can write with certainty that not a single prediction of the End has come true. Not one. Not even close.

Though it's quite possible that many ends have come and gone, each a rehearsal for the End.

Christian humanist scholars such as Eric Voegelin, Josef Pieper, and Thomas Molnar did much to prepare the world for the end of the 20th century and what would amount to barely contained lunacy regarding the End.

Thomas Molnar, reputed to be a rather unfriendly but equally brilliant man, tied the End to the beginning. If we're not focused on the End, we delude ourselves into believing we can build the Kingdom of God in the here and now. We look to the heavens, and we pull the most important things down to this world. In *Utopia: The Perennial Heresy*, Molnar wrote:

> From time to time the belief spreads among men that it is possible to construct an ideal society. Then the call is sounded for all to gather and build it—the city of God on earth. Despite its attractiveness, this is a delirious ideal stamped with the madness of logic. The truth is that society is always unfinished, always in motion, and its key problems can never be solved by social engineering. Yet, man must conquer, again and again, the freedom to see this truth. In the intervals he succumbs to the dream of a mankind frozen and final in its planetary pride.

Mystic rhythms. Without the mysticism. Just lots of rhythm. But no method.

Of those books at the end of the last century that took a look at what might happen during the End, the best fiction book is Michael O'Brien's *Father Elijah: An Apocalypse*. It comes as a part of a series of six novels O'Brien authored, collectively called *Children of the Last Days*. Unlike the *Left Behind* series, which is essentially hate-filled tripe not worthy of even being pulp, *Children of the Last Days* offers a beautiful examination of the most pressing of human questions: What is man? What is God? What is man's relationship to man? What is man's duty to God? Four of the books combine to form one story: *Sophia House* (2005); *Father Elijah* (1996); *Children of the Sun* (1998); and *Plague Journal* (1999). The other two, *Strangers and Sojourners* (1997) and *A Cry of Stone* (2003), offer us glimpses in the struggle of grace and anti-grace in the time leading up to the End. In terms of literary style and contribution to North American letters, *Sophia House* is by far the best. Set primarily in a Polish bookstore during the Nazi occupation of the early 1940s, the story revolves around a young Jewish genius and a confused Catholic intellectual and artist. The dialogue resembles a westernized version of *The Brothers Karamazov* in spirit as well as literary excellence. The young boy grows up to be Father Elijah.

Why did O'Brien choose to write in the genre of apocalyptic fiction, a field filled with the best science fiction as well as notoriously the worst? "His [man's] existence is inexpressibly beautiful—and dangerous," O'Brien explains. "It is fraught with mysteries that beg to be deciphered. The Greek word *apokalypsis* means an uncovering, or revealing." In other words, the End allows us to look at the most fundamental aspects of existence. "Through such revelations man gazes into the panorama of human history in search of the key to his identity."

Of everything I've read in the world of fiction and fantasy regarding the End, O'Brien makes the most sense. Not only is he worth reading, his ideas are worth pondering.

And, if you're looking for an excellent analysis of the whole movement from an intelligent perspective, turn to Carl Olson's *Will Catholics Be Left Behind?*

So, is it the End? Possibly. Christians have been worried about the End since the days that Christ walked the earth. Could it happen three minutes after you've read this? Maybe. Could it happen three thousand years after you read this? Just as likely.

A chapter about the End can't just end. It must End. So, I'll conclude with the words of that mighty wielder of the pen G. K. Chesterton. I'll believe his words to be true long before I succumb to the Campings and their ilk.

> *For the White Horse knew England*
> *When there was none to know;*

Mythic Realms

He saw the first oar break or bend,
He saw heaven fall and the world end,
O God, how long ago.

For the end of the world was long ago,
And all we dwell to-day
As children of some second birth,
Like a strange people left on earth
After a judgment day.

Part III: Film & the Moral Imagination

John Ford's *Stagecoach*

In 1939, John Ford released *Stagecoach*, a learned and perceptive cinematic work of art that not only introduced John Wayne as a major player in Hollywood but also made the western something more than a mere backdrop for pulp-ish adventure stories. Indeed, the movie shows that the western can serve as the perfect setting for a high-cultured morality play, mythic in its significance and its import. Themes of justice, belonging (and alienation), and redemption permeate the movie at every level.

Not surprisingly, given the title of the movie, *Stagecoach* follows the journey of a single stagecoach from Tonto, Arizona, to Lordsburg, Arizona, with three stops along the way: a way station; a small Mexican settlement; and a ferry. Always in the background looms the picturesque and stark Monument Valley.

The movie opens in Tonto, a lively and prosperous western settlement that is attempting to drive out its town physician, Dr. Boone, and its prostitute, Dallas. A gray, dull group of stern and puritanical women, the "Ladies of the Law and Order League," are on the verge of forming a mob, forcing Boone and Dallas to leave the town as quickly as possible, with a distorted version of "Shall We Meet Down by the River" offering the moody and quirky soundtrack to the moment. Boone confides in his friend and ally Dallas, noting that they are both the "victims of social prejudice."

Meanwhile, news has arrived that the Apache leader Geronimo has once again jumped the reservation and is declaring war throughout the Arizona Territory. A quick shot of the town banker, Mr. Gatewood, reveals that he is stealing money from his own bank, as he assures two employees, "What's good for the banks is good for the country."

The stagecoach, just about to leave town, despite the threats from the Apache, represents American society in every aspect. The local marshall, Curly, rides shotgun, protecting the stagecoach's driver, Buck, and their passengers. The passengers include, of course, Boone and Dallas (forced to leave, regardless of danger), a whiskey drummer from Kansas City, Kansas (Mr. Peacock, though everyone refers to him as the Reverend), and, critically, the seemingly ill wife of an army officer, a high-class lady from Virginia (Mrs. Mallory). As the stagecoach departs, a notorious southern gambler, Mr. Hatfield, attaches himself as "protection for the lady," and, just as the stagecoach is about to exit town, Gatewood—now illegally in possession of the bank's money—joins in a getaway attempt, knowing that the telegraph lines have been cut by the Apaches.

En route, Ringo "Henry" Kid (John Wayne) hitches a ride, having broken out of prison to avenge the killings of his father and brother in Lordsburg. Whatever his crimes, the Kid is clearly appreciated for his honesty and his good skills.

One must marvel at this little moving society: a lawman, a goof (the driver), an escaped criminal, a drunken physician, a prostitute, a salesman, a gambler, a criminal banker, and a Southern lady. Sides quickly form, with the Southern lady, the gambler, and the banker allied against the physician and the prostitute. Stuck in the middle of this is the salesman, whom everyone dismisses as a nobody. Yet, critically for the entire story and plot of the movie, the Kid sees no distinction between the two women, considering them both ladies and worthy of all respect. In his profound innocence and goodness, this escaped convict sees only the human person, not the trappings of social class or sin.

At first stop on the trail, no relief troops are to be found, and the cavalry that has accompanied them thus far has orders to depart. Unprotected, the members of the stagecoach decide to vote on whether they should push onto Lordsburg or return to Tonto. After some discussion of the trip, every member gets a vote.

At this vote, though, several things occur that will have serious implications for the rest of the story. First, the Kid, once again in his innocence, holds a seat for Dallas and even addresses her as "ma'am." When the gambler Hatfield votes, however, he superstitiously pulls out a card from a deck, the Ace of Spades, the symbol of death.

Voting to continue to Lordsburg, the stagecoach's second stop is at a small Mexican settlement. Chris, the owner, a devout Catholic, is married to an Apache woman, and, it turns out, Mrs. Mallory was not ill at all, but on the verge of giving birth. The stagecoach ride has jarred the baby, and with the crucial help of Dallas and a sobered-up Boone, she successfully delivers a baby girl.

The Kid is so impressed with Dallas's calm and her knowledge that he sees her now not just as a lady, but fully as a woman. As he watches her hold the baby, he falls in love. When the Kid admits his feelings and asks Dallas to marry him, though, she becomes confused and frustrated, assuming that the Kid really has no idea that she is a prostitute and, therefore, unredeemable.

As Dallas continues to nurse Mrs. Mallory back to full strength, the party once again has to decide whether to continue to Lordsburg or return to Tonto. When Dallas and the Kid talk again, she begs him to return to Tonto, knowing that he will face nothing but violence and, almost certainly, his own death while taking revenge in Lordsburg. Famously, the Kid responds in a line that Wayne would carry with him (and his reputation) to his dying days: "There are some things a man just can't run away from."

When they spot Apache war signals, they realize they have no choice. They must get to Lordsburg as quickly as possible.

The stagecoach finds that the third stop between Tonto and Lordsburg, the ferry, has already been attacked and destroyed by the Apache, and it's only a matter of time before the Apache strike them. When the stagecoach enters a huge, open expanse in Monument Valley, the Apache attack, and a massive firefight erupts. An arrow wounds Peacock, the salesman, and a bullet kills Hatfield. Just as the members of the stagecoach run out of ammo, the cavalry arrives.

The plot and the plot strands of *Stagecoach* all resolve, rather brilliantly, when the stagecoach finally makes it to Lordsburg. Once there, Dallas presents the baby to the town, and the ladies nod to her in appreciation. Peacock invites her to visit his family in Kansas City, and Mrs. Mallory expresses her gratitude. Dallas has become, almost, acceptable in society.

The town law shows up at the stagecoach, but, rather than arrest the Kid, as expected, they arrest the banker, Gatewood, noting that he foolishly did not expect the telegraph lines to be fixed. The Kid, it seems, has been forgiven. With three bullets for his rifle, the Kid fights and honorably kills the three brothers who had murdered his father and his brother.

The movie concludes with Curly and Boone sending the Kid and Dallas off to their future, to be married, and to live out their lives on the Kid's inherited ranch. Redemption and justice reign at every level. As the Kid and Dallas drive off, Boone offers the last words of the movie: "We have saved them from the blessings of civilization."

Alfred Hitchcock's *Rope*

Rope begins deceptively, with fine lilting music and scenes of an idyllic New York City block. A woman walks her baby in a stroller, a car glides down the one-way street, a policeman escorts two boys through the light traffic. Despite the omnipresent brick, glass, and concrete, the view, bizarrely, is almost pastoral. Then, as the credits finish, a fierce scream is heard, but all too briefly. The scene changes, and two young men in a plush Manhattan apartment are strangling a third.

"Strangulation has more vivid pictorial qualities," the director, Alfred Hitchcock, explained in macabre detail. "It is considerably more horrifying to watch a man struggle and strain under the agonizing pressure of an effective throttling than to see one slump and flow with bullets in his midriff or a shiv between his ribs."

The task completed, the two stuff the body of the third into a chest. Exhausted and exhilarated, one of them sighs deeply and lights a cigarette, while the other stares in stunned bewilderment and confusion. Not only have they just murdered their close friend, David Kentley, but they have also invited his family, his fiancé, his closest friend, and their old house master from prep school to a dinner party to be held almost immediately after the murder. They even serve dinner from the top of the chest as the body lies within.

"Good Americans usually die young on the battlefield, don't they?" the smug one asks, rhetorically. "The Davids of this world merely occupy space, which is why he was the perfect victim for the perfect murder. Of course, he was a Harvard undergraduate. That might make it justifiable homicide," he jokes.

The rest of the story, based on a play by Patrick Hamilton, *Rope's End*—itself based on a real-life murder from 1929—follows the several participants of the dinner party in real time. That is, the action of the movie takes place entirely within a continuous 85 minutes in the evening. Alfred Hitchcock admitted the whole idea was a bit of experiment, as each scene in the movie—with not a single break outside of the opening two-shot—happens in 10–11 minute segments, exactly the time possible per canister of film.

> I undertook *Rope* as a stunt; that's the only way I can describe it. I really don't know how I came to indulge in it. The stage drama was played out in the actual time of the story; the action is continuous from the moment the curtain goes up until it comes down again. I asked myself whether it was technically possible to film it in the same way. The only way to achieve that, I found, would be to handle the shooting in the same continuous action, with no break in the telling of the story that begins at seven-thirty and ends at nine-fifteen. And I got this crazy idea to do it in a single shot.

Almost as important, *Rope* is Hitchcock's first color movie. Color was no mere gimmick for the great director, but rather a necessity to highlight the dramatic qualities of the murder and the story falling into twilight and, ultimately, the dark night. "I wouldn't make a Technicolor picture just for the sake of using color," Hitchcock admitted. "I've waited 17 years to find a story of my type in which color actually plays a dramatic role." The employment of color was, Hitchcock said, all about mood. "We must bear in mind that, fundamentally, there's no such thing as color; in fact, there's no such thing as a face, because until the light hits it, it is non-existent," Hitchcock said. "There is no such thing as a line; there's only the light and the shade."

Hitchcock not only directed the movie, but—through his new but short-lived company Transatlantic Pictures—produced it as well. Sadly, though, *Rope* failed to show well at the box office, and the reviews of it at the time were mixed. "At all events, the picture takes on a dull tone as it goes and finally ends in a fizzle which is forecast almost from the start," lamented the *New York Times* in 1948. Less prestigious papers, such as the *Syracuse Post Standard*, claimed *Rope* held "some of the best acting, directing and photography in Technicolor that has recently slipped across the local screen," and the *Abilene Reporter News* proclaimed, "the expert use of Technicolor and Hitchcock's wizardry at building a plot to explosive excitement make *Rope* one of the screen's most sensational films."

Looking back over the history of moviemaking, it's extremely difficult for any cinephile to understand the *New York Times*'s dismissal of the film. Not only is *Rope* a great Alfred Hitchcock movie, but it has to be one of the greatest movies in cinematic history. The directing is compelling, the acting is extraordinary, the dialogue is crisp, and the unraveling of the arrogance of the murderers is downright gripping.

In hindsight, it's also impossible not to be struck by how objectively moral the story is. As teenagers, the two murderers had spent many late-night hours discussing ethics and morality with their house master, Rupert Cadell (Jimmy Stewart). He, being a follower of Friedrich Nietzsche (1844–1900), had taught them that morality and ethics existed only to keep the masses in check. The elite—or the supermen—were not only above and beyond good and evil, but had the privilege of acting as such, not just believing it. After all, the victims are "inferior beings whose lives are unimportant anyway." And who, then, are the elite? "The few are those men of such intellectual and cultural superiority that they're above the traditional moral concepts. Good and evil, right and wrong are invented for the ordinary, average man, the inferior man, because he needs them."

When Cadell figures out what his two former students have done, the reality of his teaching and philosophy becomes unbearable to him.

Justice, it seems, is absolute. So is the greatness of Alfred Hitchcock's *Rope*.

Alfred Hitchcock's *Vertigo*

Like all his best movies, Alfred Hitchcock's *Vertigo* (1958) brutally analyzes modernity, finding it schizophrenic and wanting. Unlike the stripped-down minimalism of *Rope*, which also stars Jimmy Stewart, however, *Vertigo* is in every way lush and voluptuous. The movie relies on setting and mood more than dialogue. And, unlike the confined space of the upper-class Manhattan apartment in *Rope*, *Vertigo* centers on a very middle-class detective in San Francisco. Symbols abound in the movie—symbols of American antiquity, of American nobility, of American industrialism, of American Hispanicism, and of American Catholicism. If *Rope* is philosophical, *Vertigo* is equally psychological.

Though critics loved *Vertigo* when it first appeared in 1958—the *New York Times* especially lauding it as a masterful work of cinematic art—the public, by and large, ignored it. Hitchcock, deeply embarrassed by its box-office failure, blamed Jimmy Stewart's age as no longer appealing to the public. And, strangely, *Vertigo* disappeared, becoming one of Hitchcock's so-called "lost movies." In 1983, it finally appeared again in movie theaters and, a year later, on home video. Since its re-release in the early 1980s, critics have generally considered it one of the two greatest movies ever made, vying for first place with *Citizen Kane*.

No matter how many times one watches *Vertigo*, it demands full attention and immersion. This is simply not the kind of movie that can serve as background wallpaper. It is a full work of art, and, as such, it demands everything of us. Even the opening credits—disturbingly Freudian and Jungian—disorient the viewer. Designed by famed animator Saul Bass, they consist of swirling designs, taking us into the eye and the mind—depths of psychological despair, horror—of a personal and existential abyss. It should also serve as a warning. If you watch this movie believing you'll end two hours later with a smile on your face and in your heart, you will be sorely mistaken. There's nothing happy about this movie.

Past the opening credits, the opening scene is now an absolute classic as several men run across the rooftops of San Francisco at dusk, a scene imitated by *Dark City* and *The Matrix*. Just as the chase begins, detective John "Scotty" Ferguson (Jimmy Stewart) slips, holding onto a drainage pipe for dear life. As a fellow police officer tries to aid Scotty, vertigo strikes the detective, allowing his would-be helper and colleague to fall several stories down, dying upon impact with the ground. An official inquiry clears Scotty of any wrongdoing, but, wracked with guilt, he quits the police department. This is a huge fall for Scotty, as he had been a lawyer turned detective, hoping one day to become San Francisco police commissioner.

Scotty's best friend is Midge, his longtime and presumably only girlfriend, who called off their engagement sometime during college, but who still clearly loves him. That she loves Scotty is clear, but how she loves him remains unclear throughout the movie. A professional seamstress and designer, Midge streamlines and engineers bras. As with so much in Hitchcock, the sexual orientation of the characters is unclear. In *Rope*, the killers are almost certainly homosexual. In *Vertigo*, Midge might very well be a lesbian, though this is far from obvious. She reveals herself to be overly protective of Scotty, though she's fine with him remaining romantically unattached. When he shows interest in another woman, Midge becomes excessively possessive, though she's still not willing to give a serious and committed relationship with him a chance.

Another old college friend re-enters his life after the end of Scotty's hospitalization. Armed with a strangely convoluted story about ghosts, past lives, and spiritual hauntings, he asks Scotty to follow his wife—who is supposedly possessed by a Hispanic beauty of 19th-century San Francisco, Carlotta Valdez. Toward the end of her tragic life, the fallen beauty Carlotta descended into madness, asking for her child while wandering aimlessly through the streets of San Francisco. The old college friends claims to fear that his wife is also descending into madness.

As mentioned earlier in this chapter, everything is lush in *Vertigo*. In *Rope*, everything is claustrophobic. Here, in *Vertigo*, everything is huge, open, and dizzying. It's hard to get one's bearings in the movie, an obvious intention on the part of the director. Hitchcock famously hated filming outside. A perfectionist, he wanted control over every aspect of the film. Much of *Vertigo*, however, takes place in the outdoors, and Hitchcock proves himself as adept at outdoor filmmaking as indoor, despite his own hesitations. Again, details abound in *Vertigo*, often overly crowding the screen. Hitchcock even hired Edith Head—perhaps immortalized in our generation best as the outrageous designer of *The Incredibles*—to tailor and customize all of the women's outfits in the film. Voluptuous in its varied scapes, San Francisco serves as the perfect backdrop to the film.

Without giving away too many plot details—all of which are unexpected, twisting and turning in ways perhaps only logical to the perplexing soul of Hitchcock—we can say that *Vertigo* follows pretended madness as well as real madness. There's a murder central to the story, and Scotty, once again, finds himself caught in the middle, unsure of his own longings, his own virtues, and his own sins.

Perhaps most importantly, however, Scotty falls in love for the second time in his life. Midge might have been first, but the new woman—played by Kim Novak—becomes Scotty's rather unhealthy obsession. Novak has deceived the much older man, and he has fallen for her completely. As first, she presents herself as an upper-class platinum blond, as sophisticated as possibly imaginable in the 1950s. Later, in the film, she offers herself as a lonely and morally suspect transplant from Salina, Kansas. Now, far from the platinum blond, she is a rather sexualized redneck, a bumpkin making her way in the big city. Scotty falls for both, recognizing the possibilities of remaking the redhead into the platinum blond.

As mentioned earlier, one should not enter this movie lightly or with the expectation of a happy ending. As many times as I've watched this movie over the last thirty years, it never fails to depress me. It also, obviously, intrigues me to no end. This is not a simple work of art. This is deep, nuanced, and layered. Each viewing reveals something deep and profound.

As with the story being a whirligig of convoluted desires, so too is the morality of *Vertigo*. Whatever Hitchcock thought after the movie's box-office failure, Stewart's performance is impeccable. As is Barbara Bel-Geddes's portrayal of Midge. If there's a problem with the film, it's Kim Novak. By 1950s standards, she might have been considered attractive. For me, she just looks cheap and sleazy. Had Jimmy Stewart been any less of an actor, his obsession with Novak would be laughable. Fortunately, he is the perfect male lead of the 1950s. Equal parts wily and innocent, equal parts tough and vulnerable.

Regardless, *Vertigo* remains a gem, one of the truly great works of art of the last century.

Alfred Hitchcock's *The Birds*

"I am neither poor nor innocent"—Melanie Daniels, protagonist of Hitchcock's *The Birds*

Cinema as Art

From the time I was thirteen or so, I fell deeply in love with movies. I did not grow up watching a lot of TV shows, but I certainly loved renting movies and enjoying them in the comfort of my house, especially when my parents were out playing bridge or doing something similar with their friends.

For me—then and now—the more intense the movie, the better, though I also loved stupid, slapstick comedies. Several of my high school friends appreciated and understood the actual art of cinema far more than I did, and I learned a great deal from them about directors, cuts, camera angles, actors, lighting. Even to this day, I can't watch anything other than comedy without analyzing every aspect of the film.

College didn't give me much time for movies, but two events in graduate school not only re-awakened my passion but increased it exponentially. The first, and less important of the two, was the attending of a film studies class on the 1956 version of *Invasion of the Body Snatchers*. Everything my friends in high school had taught me was sharpened to a finely and intellectually honed blade of finest steel as the professor explained how to study a film, scene by scene—the method similar to the examination of a novel, but with a different kind of depth.

Hitchcock, His Women, and Me

Additionally, in graduate school, two friends really shaped my view on films. The first was Craig, an apartment-mate as well as office buddy. As it turned out, Craig knew British film really well. I'd never appreciated it or PBS before, but he gave me that love of both. Second, I found out that another close friend was also an Alfred Hitchcock (1899–1980) fanatic. Tamzen (my great friend to this day) and I spent many hours watching and analyzing Hitchcock. These moments with Craig and Tamzen are ones I still treasure.

Like Tamzen, I considered myself a Hitchcock fanatic as well, preferring a Hitchcock film even to a science fiction one. I especially loved, in order, *Rope*, *Vertigo*, *Psycho*, *Strangers on a Train*, and *North by Northwest*. I also watched other Hitchcock films, such as *Topaz*, *Marnie*, *Frenzy*, *The Man Who Knew Too Much*, but I generally considered these films relatively normal as opposed to the aforementioned.

In each of these, whether of the highest caliber or merely of the good caliber, Hitchcock masterfully demonstrated his genius. In each, he picked exactly the right actors, the right stories, and the right actors for the stories, and the right stories for the actors. He took his time and lingered—over a shot or a conversation—where needed, and he added drama where needed. Almost all his films revolved around some sin, some guilt, and some penance. His films are truly Catholic theology on the silver screen. His Jesuit education comes across in every frame of film.

The Puzzle of *The Birds*

The movie that has intrigued me more than any other is *The Birds*. By "intrigued," I mean that I find watching it a true intellectual challenge, a puzzle to be solved, rather than a work of art to enjoy. As far as I can tell, it does not possess the intellectual depth of *Rope* or the psychological dread of *Vertigo* or the confessional aspect of *Psycho*. Yet it intrigues me. A lot.

For the longest time, I was convinced that the film best represents the very Roman Catholic Alfred Hitchcock's views on feminism. The women of the film, after all, are fascinating. They are powerful and cunning (Tippi Hedren), insecure and frightened (Jessica Tandy), or cool and resigned (Suzanne Pleshette). The leading man (Rod Taylor) is a smart aleck and, more or less, heroic, but he is rather uninspiring. Whether this is because he wasn't a great actor or Hitchcock wanted him to be this way, I have no idea. Frankly, he's just not that interesting.

But the women? Absolutely interesting. They make the movie in every possible way.

Is *The Birds* about feminism? I don't know, and I'm less convinced of this now than I was a decade ago. Hitchcock's film is, however, about femininity. It is also, at some level, a commentary on nature: nature as nature; nature as revenge; nature as law superior to human contrivance; nature, red in tooth and claw.

The film begins in a pristine-looking San Francisco, wealthy people moving about their business. Filmed only a half-decade before the drug culture would thrive in the city, this San Francisco seems a million miles away from our time. This is most assuredly not the San Francisco of *Dirty Harry* or of the 1978 version of *The Invasion of the Body Snatchers*. No grit here. Only wealth and confidence.

Melanie Daniels (Tippi Hedren), graced with perfect looks and class, walks into a pet shop specializing in birds. She has ordered an exotic bird that has yet to arrive in the shop. As she waits, a dashing man, Mitch Brenner (Rod Taylor), presumes she works there and asks a question about love birds. She attempts to bluff her way through the conversation but fails. After a bit of repartee, she concedes defeat. The following day, after getting his personal information from his license plate, she decides to drive to Bodega Bay with the love birds, hoping to surprise him. She succeeds in this, and the two begin a flirtatious game, clearly attracted to one another while pretending not to be. Daniels encounters two women almost immediately: Lydia Brenner (Jessica Tandy), Taylor's overly protective and suspicious mom; and his cool but resigned ex-girlfriend, Annie Hayworth (Suzanne Pleshette). Headstrong, selfish, and spoiled, Daniels works her way into the lives of each.

As Daniels and Hayworth talk over brandy, they realize that Mitch has drawn them each there, but his mother has repelled them both as well. Still, Hayworth admits to liking Mitch so much she's willing to stay in Bodega Bay, simply to be Mitch's friend.

As Daniels continues navigating her way into Brenner's family, birds of a variety of different species begin to attack individuals and then groups in Bodega Bay, normally an idyllic spot on the Pacific Coast. Daniels is the first to be attacked, but soon schoolchildren and then the general population come under attack.

Despite making and releasing the movie in 1963, Hitchcock creates some truly terrifying and brutal scenes. When the birds attack, blood often flies freely, eyes get gouged out, and corpses litter the ground. None of it is gratuitous, but it is graphic. Hayworth's broken body is particularly gruesome.

For some reason that the protagonists cannot fathom, the birds—though of different species—offer concentrated and coordinated attacks.

The finale of the movie revolves around the boarding-up of a nice home (the home of Brenner, his younger sister, and his mom) and the attempt to hold off the concerted avian onslaught.

In one memorable and deeply troubling scene, birds break into the attic just as Daniels is there, trying to secure the house. They ravage her. The filming was so intense that Hedren had to spend a week in a local hospital recovering from the trauma and exhaustion.

Just as quickly at the birds became violent, they become quiescent, as their night of violence draws to a close. Neither Hitchcock nor his film ever explains the behavior of the birds. Instead, we see only the reaction of the humans. That Hitchcock leaves the motives totally unexplained makes the movie only creepier. The movie concludes with Brenner, Daniels, and Brenner's mom and sister walking through hordes of birds, all quiet now, and leaving Bodega Bay by car. Daniels has been so traumatized by the events of the day that she is catatonic. Brenner's mother, having been suspicious of Daniels from the beginning, now accepts her, cradling her as though her daughter.

The movie ends, with no music, as the four drive into the sunrise, the birds cawing but staying put. The viewer is left with really nothing. With no music cues and a flat shot of the car departing the fields of birds, the audience has no way of knowing whether Brenner and company drive into death or into safety.

The movie just ends.

Whether the movie is about existentialism, about the bombings of London in World War II, about feminism, or about the sovereignty of nature, I have no idea. Well, lots of ideas, but no certainties. Yet, like all Hitchcock movies—this one taken from a short story—it continues to fascinate and to titillate.

The Essences of *Dr. Strangelove*

We must do everything possible to protect our bodily fluids. After all, the human body is mostly water. If one's water becomes corrupt, his "essences" will follow, and man will lose what power he possesses. He must, no matter the cost, protect his "purity of essence." So raves General Jack D. Ripper throughout the first two-thirds of Stanley Kubrick's dark comedy and historical mocumentary of the future, *Dr. Strangelove or: How I Learned to Stop Worrying and Love the Bomb.*

> General Jack D. Ripper [Sterling Hayden]: But today, war is too important to be left to politicians. They have neither the time, the training, nor the inclination for strategic thought. I can no longer sit back and allow Communist infiltration, Communist indoctrination, Communist subversion and the international Communist conspiracy to sap and impurify all of our precious bodily fluids.

The film originally appeared in theaters only a month and a week after the Kennedy assassination (at one point, an Air Force major explaining that the emergency survival kit would allow any survivor to have a "good time in Dallas" is dubbed to state "a good time in Vegas"; otherwise, the film was left as is) and almost certainly affected significant aspects of the 1964 presidential campaign, especially through the infamous ad of the little girl picking flower petals with a nuclear bomb detonating.

> Major King Kong [Slim Pickens]: Survival kit contents check. In them you'll find: one forty-five caliber automatic; two boxes of ammunition; four days' concentrated emergency rations; one drug issue containing antibiotics, morphine, vitamin pills, pep pills, sleeping pills, tranquilizer pills; one miniature combination Russian phrase book and Bible; one hundred dollars in rubles; one hundred dollars in gold; nine packs of chewing gum; one issue of prophylactics; three lipsticks; three pair of nylon stockings. Shoot, a fella' could have a pretty good weekend in [Vegas] with all that stuff.

While the president of the United States in the film looks more than a little bit like Adlai Stevenson, intelligent and kind but ultimately effete, several of the military officers could be Goldwater or Johnson in both appearance and speaking style. While the film is deeply political in a broad sense, it's really not political in the immediate sense. That is, Kubrick lambasts every side of things—left, right, capitalist, communist, above, below, near, and through.

Only one character in the entire film comes across well, a polite and increasingly determined British officer, serving as an ExO on an American military base. He was, it turns out, a sound warrior in the Asian theater of World War II, captured and tortured by the Japanese but now somewhat taken with their ability to innovate and produce consumer products. Appropriately, Kubrick names him Group Captain Lionel Mandrake.

> Lionel Mandrake [Peter Sellers]: Do I look all rancid and clotted? You look at me, Jack. Eh? Look, eh? And I drink a lot of water, you know. I'm what you might call a water man, Jack—that's what I am. And I can swear to you, my boy, swear to you, that there's nothing wrong with my bodily fluids. Not a thing, Jackie.

Others in the film carry much more unflattering names: President Merkin Muffley, General Jack D. Ripper, Colonel Bat Guano, Soviet Premier Kissoff, and Russian Ambassador de Sadesky.

It's not just the names, though. American soldiers work in sterile, modern environments, surrounded by computers and masses of paper. The lighting in every room is neon, artificial, and harsh. American pilots, though the most professional in the movie, look at *Playboy*, mess with cards, chew bubble gum, and eat endless amounts of candy bars and donuts. The military officers crave power openly, and the politicians drink, whore, and bluster.

The Half-Century Mark

Now beyond the half-century mark, *Dr. Strangelove* deserves some scrutiny and some praise. Only four years younger than the film, I first saw it in the fall of 1987 in a movie theater in Innsbruck, Austria. The version I saw, dubbed in German, left me astonished. What struck me most, however, was that whoever dubbed the movie into

German chose to use an Austrian with a dense Tyrolean accent for Slim Pickens's deeply thick Texas accent. When I returned to the United States the following year, I watched it again, this time in English.

> Major King Kong [Slim Pickens]: Well, boys, I reckon this is it—nuclear combat toe to toe with the Russkies. Now look, boys, I ain't much of a hand at makin' speeches, but I got a pretty fair idea that something doggone important is goin' on back there. And I got a fair idea the kinda personal emotions that some of you fellas may be thinkin'. Heck, I reckon you wouldn't even be human bein's if you didn't have some pretty strong personal feelin's about nuclear combat. I want you to remember one thing, the folks back home is a-countin' on you and by golly, we ain't about to let 'em down. I tell you something else, if this thing turns out to be half as important as I figure it just might be, I'd say that you're all in line for some important promotions and personal citations when this thing's over with. That goes for ever' last one of you regardless of your race, color or your creed. Now let's get this thing on the hump—we got some flyin' to do.

Mostly inspired by the number of references the famous economist Bob Higgs makes to the movie on social media, I decided to watch it attentively and with an eye toward deconstruction and explanation. What power does this work of art hold?

I watched it from the opening moment to the end with my full attention. Indeed, it's the kind of movie that mesmerizes and hypnotizes. It lures the watcher in seductively with its driving, unrelenting plot, demanding acceptance rather than leavening imagination. If for no other reason, Kubrick deserves praise for creating a film that serves the role of cult leader, taking in his deluded worshippers. For 95 minutes last night, I allowed myself to be that follower, and I allowed myself to be submerged in the film. Like any religion or ideology, it cannot be understood except as from within.

Phallic Power

While *Dr. Strangelove* contains a number of extremely hilarious moments and some of the best "over-the-top" acting imaginable (Peter Sellers, George C. Scott, and Slim Pickens), it is the driving and unrelenting plot of the story that captivates the viewer. The story ends in the destruction of the world. *Dr. Strangelove*, however, is an allegory about man's desire (and pubescent fantasy) to control the world through phallic sexuality. Tellingly, only one woman appears in the entire film. She's the secretary and lover of George C. Scott's character, General Buck Turgidson. The viewer first encounters her as a real person as she lounges in her bikini under a sunbathing lamp in the general's swank bedroom. He's answering the call of nature in the restroom, and she takes an emergency call at 3 in the morning. We also see her one other time, as the playmate in the *Playboy* a bomber pilot is reading. In the magazine, she is lying across some kind of bear rug, and a copy of the journal *Foreign Affairs*—containing an article by Henry Kissinger—covers her rear end. At no other times in the 95 minutes of the movie does a woman appear. Even signs in the background, posted at military bases, appeal only to the vigilance of fathers to protect their children.

The movie itself begins with some gorgeous filming of a B52 being refueled in flight. The movement and sway of the planes as they connect to one another clearly reflects the act of sexual intercourse. Yet it is "Strangelove," as both planes, of course, look phallic and certainly not vaginal. Once decoupled, or released, the B52 crew, led by Slim Pickens, flies without hesitation toward its target. It is, for all intents and purposes, a single sperm in search of an egg to fertilize.

Led by patriot Pickens, the crew members—including a very young James Earl Jones—follows their instructions professionally even as they unceasingly chew gum. Kubrick presents them as young, uninspired technocrats. Yet, in the end, Pickens rides the nuclear bomb all the way down to Soviet soil in rodeo style, seemingly loving the glory of it all.

The movie ends with explosive orgasm, an orgasm so fierce that it destroys the surface of the entire world even as it fertilizes.

An escaped Nazi-turned-American, Dr. Strangelove, has, however, planned for all eventualities. For the leaders of the Free World—all men, of course—decide to accept Strangelove's advice and move into underground bunkers. There, they will possess 10 wives each (thus undoing Christian norms in the name of survival) and produce a eugenic super-race to reemerge a century later to reconquer the world.

Throughout the movie, the U.S. president moves from horror at the possibility of the destruction of the world to relaxed acceptance of the ten women awaiting him in his own private Apocalypse.

A Profound Cultural Moment

Over five decades later, it would be difficult to underplay the importance or staying power of *Dr. Strangelove*.

Though most remember it for just a very few lines and hand gestures offered by Dr. Strangelove, played by Sellers, it is really George C. Scott who steals the show. His Shatner-esque over-the-top acting works perfectly. Most importantly, the viewer can see the subtle and not so subtle changes in his Machiavellian soul and thought through his body language, his voice intonations, and his facial expressions. Probably the best and most hilarious moment of the entire film is the call Scott's character receives from his secretary and lover during his meeting with the president. Though Scott attempts to assure his lover quietly, it is clear the entire room can hear the conversation but awkwardly chooses not to respond.

Over the phone, he assures the bathing beauty that he will make her his wife soon and that he believes his relationship to her more important than his duty to the president. Best of all, he ends the conversation by reminding his lover to say her prayers before calling it a night.

Even if more than a bit diabolic in some of his artistry, Stanley Kubrick offered a post-Vietnam and post-Watergate cynicism a decade early. By 1974, even the most loyal Americans would question the integrity of the military and the government. But, in 1964, only five weeks after the murder of a president in a Texas city, *Dr. Strangelove* shocked an American public emerging from a naive innocence and standing at the very cusp of a cultural revolution.

Star Trek and Friendship

As young children, my older brother and I watched the original *Star Trek* series on Saturday mornings. We weren't big TV watchers as a family, but *Star Trek* was special. To make it even better, it was the local PBS that aired *Star Trek*, presenting it free of all commercials.

Every Saturday, Todd and I awoke very early and watched the rerun for that week. This would have been around 1975, almost a decade after the show first aired. After each episode, Todd and I would talk, always mesmerized by the possibilities of space, life, and a billion other things. How much of the galaxy had this crew explored? Were they the modern Lewis & Clark? What happened when someone transported from one place to another? How smart were the computers? Were the Klingons the Soviets and the Romulans the Chinese? Or maybe the other way around? Why did we only see the military aspects of Starfleet? What about the colonists, the pioneers? How did time travel work? If the Enterprise found itself sent back to Earth, why did it happen to arrive the same year the show was being filmed?

Pretty serious stuff for an eight-year-old sitting with his much admired thirteen-year-old brother.

I had no idea at the time, but the show's founder and creator, Gene Roddenberry, had actually described *Star Trek* as a "wagon train to the stars" when he first shopped it to studios. It would be set, though, on the space equivalent of an aircraft carrier, a mobile community as diverse as *Gunsmoke*'s Dodge City, he continued in his show treatment. The crew, roughly 203 of them, would be as diverse as possible, asserting that racial prejudice and ethnic strife would be things of the past in the non-specified time of *Star Trek*. Only later did the show writers decide it took place in the 2260s. From its beginning, however, Roddenberry's *Star Trek* represented a brash Kennedy-esque liberalism, a confidence that America could teach the world the principles of civilization, tolerance, and dignity.

And yet, this wouldn't be merely a western in space. Roddenberry recruited some of the finest science fiction and horror talent available in the 1960s, including D.C. Fontana, David Gerrold, Robert Bloch, Samuel Peeples, Richard Matheson, Theodore Sturgeon, and Harlan Ellison. Ray Bradbury also served as an advisor to the show.

Though much of *Star Trek* now appears campy, especially with its poor attempts at humor and terrible costumes (especially for the aliens), there's no doubt the team making the show took science fiction and its ideas very seriously. Themes of natural rights, equality, imperialism, personality, racism, religion, history, culture, and much else important in life appeared throughout the original 79 episodes. It must be noted, though, that I don't remember my young self thinking poorly of the special effects.

My favorite scene—Kirk fighting a gorn—proved way too much for my kids. "Dad," my oldest daughter asked, "why is Captain Kirk fighting a guy in a rubber suit?"

And, of course, my brother and I loved all of the fight scenes. Who wouldn't want to follow Kirk into battle? The guy was made for serious leadership. Plus, the over-the-top fight music was simply incredible. I can still recall the entire theme instantly, while poorly visualizing the yellow-shirted Kirk kicking, punching, and rolling. I'm really not sure how many times I tried to perfect Kirk's jump-kick maneuver as a child. It's amazing I'm not more damaged than I am. Thank the good Lord I only tried it upon invisible and imagined foes. I wasn't so fortunate when it came to the Vulcan nerve pinch. Practice with this—especially after sneaking up on members of my family—really only resulted in sore muscles and hurt feelings.

When it came down to the quick of it all, though, it was the interaction of the personalities—the characters of Kirk, Spock, McCoy, and Scotty, especially—on the show that meant so much to us.

Star Trek demonstrated, over and over, I think, that real heroism comes not from individualism, but from friendship. These guys on that little screen not only loved one another, but they each bettered the other.

When *Star Wars* came out in 1977, I loved it. But in no way did it compare to *Star Trek*, at least to my way of thinking. I knew that *Star Wars* was essentially science fantasy, while *Trek* was real science fiction. Again, as my young mind saw it, Luke Skywalker and Han Solo were great, but for real fantasy, I turned to Tolkien. For sci-fi, I wanted Kirk and Spock and a whole host of science fiction authors from Asimov to Clarke.

When *Star Trek: The Motion Picture* came out, my mom took me to an opening show in Kansas City—then the major metropolis in my life. We saw it right before Christmas, 1979, and I was completely blown away. The scale of it reminded me of *2001*, and the return of NASA's Voyager spacecraft for a science-loving kid was a dream come true. To top it off, the movie ended with the creation of an entirely new form of life, an incarnation of man and machine. What wasn't to love? This seemed so much better than the blowing-up of a Death Star!

Rewatching it quite recently, it hit me what a beautiful movie it is. Many critics have complained that it simply failed to have enough action, that it demanded too much of the viewer. This is all probably true, and these are also the reasons I liked the movie so much, even as a 12-year-old. *Star Trek: The Motion Picture* is a film that allows one to consider possibilities, to realize the immensity of the unknown, and to contemplate the potential dangers of space travel. The movie demands immersion.

Nothing prepared me, though, for *Star Trek II: The Wrath of Khan*. I saw it only days after my eighth-grade year ended. It hit me hard, very hard. The film is the best of the best when it comes to Star Trek. Shakespearean acting flies freely, dialogue from Melville comes equally fast, and the plot moves as dramatically as the best war movies made prior to *Apocalypse Now*. Realizing how quickly they're aging, the crew encounters a genetically engineered superman from the late 20th century, a Nietzschean tyrant bent on absolute revenge for Kirk's actions in the *Original Series* episode, "Space Seed."

Unlike every one of the later movies, *Star Trek II: The Wrath of Khan* avoids camp, managing to tell a story as serious as *Star Trek: The Motion Picture* but with immense humanity of friendship, community, and sacrifice. Shatner especially is at his best. The scene where he allows his arrogance to bring death upon his crew and the scene in which he realizes Spock has sacrificed himself for their mission are particularly moving scenes. For better or worse, I'm sure I have watched *The Wrath of Khan* more times than any other movie in my life. I have it memorized—dialogue, scenes, and music. Still, the movie has never become so familiar to me that these two scenes just described fail to move me to tears.

Star Trek III: The Search for Spock had some fine moments, but it was clear that the crew would never again reach the heights of *Wrath of Khan*. *Star Trek IV* returns to sap and camp, and the movies really become uneven from that point forward. Yet no one could deny its popularity and money-making ability. Thus far, there have been a total of five live-action television series, one animated series, and ten movies set in the original universe. Two additional movies—though essentially action films in the vein of *Star Wars*—have appeared in the rebooted timeline. One can also find *Star Trek* toys, comics, and books everywhere and anywhere.

Star Trek has permeated our consciousness as much as or more than any other manifestation of pop culture.

Why? Several reasons, but only two need be mentioned here.

First, I'm convinced its timing was most fortuitous, coming as an optimistic Kennedy-esque frontier vision just as the 1960s soured into the imperial horrors of our policy in southeast Asia, with the subsequent dramatic loss of American confidence.

Second, and more importantly, the show was about friendship, community, and sacrifice. Art, drama, and theater might very well mock or forget such themes in cynical and decadent ages, but they can never be utterly destroyed.

Kirk needed Spock, and Spock needed Kirk. The same was just as true for Scotty and McCoy. Individually, they succumbed to terrors, errors, and arrogance. As a group of friends, playing off and leavening the strengths of the other, they were unstoppable.

These are not just good lessons; they are western and, even better, transcendent ones.

The Horrors of *The Killing Fields*

In the late winter/early spring of 1985, I attended a showing of the most immersive and artful movie I had yet encountered in my life: Roland Joffe's *The Killing Fields*. Growing up in a Goldwater household in a conservative Kansas town, I was nothing if not a pure Reaganite, a student (such that only 17-year-olds can be) and hater of ideologies of the left and the right. Growing up in a rather idyllic setting, however, meant that my view of the world was rather limited. I knew how horribly the ideologues of the world treated their citizens, but I certainly had nothing but my reading to go on. I felt for the Russian people, but they were also as distant to me in central Kansas as were the Martians. I knew a lot, especially for a teenager, but it was all from books. *The Killing Fields* opened entirely new worlds to me. It made the horrors of communism palpable in ways even the greatest books could not. And it demonstrated to me—rather conclusively—that cinema as a medium can reach the level of the greatest art. I still consider it one of the single greatest movies I have ever seen, and I watch it yearly. Only weeks after watching the movie in the theater, I wrote my entrance essay for the University of Notre Dame on a "work of art that changed my life." I chose, not surprisingly, *The Killing Fields*.

Based on the true events of the life of a *New York Times* employee, Dith Pran (a native Cambodian-Khmer), who has to escape the Cambodian gulag, circa 1976, the movie follows Pran through his horrific and terrifying escape from the Khmer Rouge, a journey that took four years from beginning to end. The actor who plays Dith Pran, Dr. Haing Ngor, had experienced almost the exact same persecution and escape from his native country. Ironically, Haing Ngor escaped from Cambodia only to be mugged and murdered in the driveway of his Chinatown-Los Angeles home in 1996. The two main characters of the movie—Sidney and Pran—separate in 1975 after the fall of Phnom Penn but reunite in 1979 at the conclusion of the movie, as they did in real life.

Historical background

The Kingdom of Cambodia, a French colony, was one of the most stable countries in southeast Asia in the 1960s. Industrializing and converting, quickly, to Christianity, the country enjoyed a prosperity that eluded its neighbors, Vietnam and Laos.

In 1969, President Richard Nixon began a secret, illegal, and unconstitutional incursion into Cambodia, correctly believing that Vietnamese communists were using rural parts of the country to transport weapons from North Vietnam to South Vietnam. He ordered carpet-bombing as well as the establishment of military bases in Cambodia. The struggle between American and communist forces quickly destabilized the region, further radicalizing many of the already radical elements in the country.

The most important of the insurgents was a group of existentialist communists, the Khmer Rouge (Red Cambodians), under the leadership of Pol Pot (an assumed name and title) and his organization, The Ankor (The Organization). Pol Pot (1925–1998) was born Saloth Sar. Though a Roman Catholic and a devout Jeffersonian coming out of high school, Sar attended university in Paris, from 1949 to 1953, where he came under the influence of several Marxists, especially the radical former-Nazi-collaborator-turned-communist, philosopher Jean-Paul Sartre (1905–1980).

When Sar returned to Cambodia in 1953, he allied himself with Vietnamese communists and dedicated himself to the overthrow of western society in Cambodia, taking the name Pol Pot. He and his organization, the Ankor, led by a number of PhD students from France (all Cambodian), became the center of Marxist revolution.

Their Marxism, perhaps the most radical ever to gain power anywhere, was existentialist and anti-urban to the extreme. In a way that seems a pure contradiction to most in the West, Pol Pot fused Marx and Jefferson, taking the hatred of the wealthy from the former and the fear of cities from the latter.

When South Vietnam fell to the communists (in April 1975), and the Americans abandoned their long-time allies, Cambodia fell to the Khmer Rouge. Immediately upon taking over the country, the Khmer Rouge forced all Cambodians out of the cities, putting them to work (mostly in "make-work" projects) throughout the countryside.

Any person possessing any religious background at all, or any education past eighth grade, or foreign language skills (anything other than Khmer and French), was immediately executed. Any display of emotion—happiness, sorrow, anguish—also led to immediate execution, as emotions were defined as middle-class constructs.

During the three years the Khmer Rouge controlled the country, it murdered nearly one out of every two Cambodians in what has been named the "Killing Fields," a term that ought to elicit the same horrors as "the Gulag" and the "Holocaust camps." In comparison to the Soviets, who killed 62 million of their own citizens during their rule of Russia, the Chinese Communists, who slaughtered 65 million of their own, and the Nazis, who butchered 21 million, the number of those murdered in Cambodia, 4.5 million, may seem a pittance. But it must be remembered not only that this number represents nearly half of the entire Cambodian population, but also that these murders were committed in a mere three years.

The members of the Khmer Rouge also began to kill one another—much as the French Revolutionaries had done to one another, after 1792—in attempt to "purify" the Marxism of their own revolution. As Russell Kirk wisely noted, revolutions have a tendency to eat their own children.

Tired of the instability and unpredictability of their neighbors, the Vietnamese Communists overthrew the Khmer Rouge in 1978, establishing a puppet communist government. Pol Pot continued to wage revolution—though with little effectiveness—until his death in 1998. The United States, regrettably, even aided him from time to time, especially in the 1990s, believing him better than his Vietnamese opponents.

The Pathos of John Hughes

"'We'll never see his like again,' said economist Ben Stein, a close friend of Hughes and one of the service's speakers. 'He was the Wordsworth of the suburban America postwar generation. He was a great, great, great genius and as much of a friend and a great family man as he was a poet.'"—*Los Angeles Times* (August 12, 2009)

One of the most unsung and nearly forgotten cultural critics of the last two decades of the twentieth century was John Hughes. Born in 1950, he died of a heart attack in 2009, at the young age of 59. Raised in Michigan and Illinois, Hughes began his career writing jokes for nationally famous comedians as well as for *National Lampoon*. For nearly every person of my age group and generation (ca. age 55), he defined the 1980s. Indeed, he's as much a part of my memory of that decade as are Ronald Reagan, Rush, and *Blade Runner*. A friend of P. J. O'Rourke, with whom he wrote but never produced a film script entitled *The History of Ohio from the Beginning of Time to the End of the Universe*, Hughes successfully captured the contempt that teenagers in the 1980s had for unearned and undeserved authority.

In particular, Hughes understood how utterly hollow and meaningless the 1960s radicals were. They may have talked revolution, but when they attained positions of power, they merely desired to make the world in their own image, all of their supposed liberalism nothing but a sham, a superficial means for gaining authority. Never did they care about peace, love, or happiness. They cared only for power. Hughes's 1986 character Ferris Bueller expressed the author's own conservative views of the world rather nicely.

> It's not that I condone fascism . . . or any ism for that matter. Isms in my opinion are not good. A person should not believe in an ism. He should believe in himself. I quote John Lennon. "I don't believe in Beatles, I just believe in me." A good point there. After all, he was the walrus.

Hughes's best movies were *The Breakfast Club*; *Sixteen Candles*; *Ferris Buehler's Day Off*; *Plane, Trains, and Automobiles*; and *Home*

Alone. He also wrote a number of Christmas movies as well as children's movies for Disney and other companies. Some of his movies were simply silly, such as *Vacation, Christmas Vacation,* and *Weird Science.*

His movies were equal parts perceptive insights into the human condition, mockeries of unearned and undeserved authority, slapstick comedy, introductions to the best of popular music, examinations of tight friendships, and development of full characters. In addition to these traits and themes, Hughes almost always wrote his stories around creative persons held down by peer pressure and societal desires for conformity. His movies end happily, but not without great struggles.

Possessed of an overwhelming reclusive J.D. Salinger streak, Hughes wrote a number of screenplays, produced and directed a number of films, made lots and lots of money, and then, around 1991, disappeared from public view. While he still wrote and produced—often under the pseudonym Edmond Dantes—he avoided any publicity, preferring as much privacy as possible. By all accounts, he was a serious husband and father who put his family above his career.

The Breakfast Club (1985)

Of his numerous movies, one stands above all the rest as a true work of art: 1985's *The Breakfast Club.* Again, to address my age group and my era, it captured my longings, my hopes, and my desires more than any other movie I have ever seen. I don't mean this in the sense that it's the best movie I've ever seen or the best ever made. It doesn't compare to *The Rope, The Killing Fields, The Mission,* or even *Batman Begins.* For movies that deal with real life, though, it's a stunner. I'll never forget walking out of the theater in 1985, being so stunned that any adult could understand my peers and me as Hughes did. For all intents and purposes, it was and remains the quintessential movie of the 1980s.

I watched it so many times when it first came out and in the decade afterward that I have the movie memorized (mostly) line by line and scene by scene. The other day, while I was on a lecturing trip to Florida, the movie was playing on the video screen of the treadmill I was using. I didn't turn up the sound. I didn't need to. Every line of dialogue was in my head, and the forty-five minutes of exercise flew by as though I weren't exercising at all. The whole time, I thought about how much the movie remained a work of art and how much I missed the artistic insights that John Hughes offered the world in his own quirky way.

The Breakfast Club revolves around only seven characters, all meeting at a Chicago high school in a middle-to-upper-middle-class suburb (zip code 60062), on one Saturday, March 24, 1984.

Everything is minimalist, from the opening title sequence to the movie itself. Using almost no budget, it could have appeared just as easily as a stage play as it does a movie. Hughes wrote the movie to have almost non-stop dialogue with some action for comedic pauses and breaks from the intensity of the story.

Five students—a weirdo (Ally Sheedy), a jock (Emilio Estevez), a socialite (Molly Ringwald), a stoner (Judd Nelson), and a brain (Anthony Michael Hall)—all find themselves in detention. The only drawn-out adults in the movie are the vice principal (Paul Gleason), an arrogant and insecure opportunist, and the school janitor (John Kapelos), a lovable guy who was that high school's "man of the year" in 1969.

Most of the film takes place in the school library as the five students learn to understand one another, mostly by recognizing their own shared distaste for their teachers, their parents, and the peer pressure of their respective social groups. While the movie plays up a bit too much the sexuality as well as the drugs of the period, it also, in a very Hughes fashion, reaches toward the best of western civilization, the art and the thinkers that allow us to be where we are as a civilization, mixed with a lot of references to popular culture. It is not, after all, accidental that the movie takes place in a library, with the students surrounded by art, books, and statues.

Adversity to Harmony

The movie opens with a quote from David Bowie:

And these children that you spit on
As they try to change their world

Are immune to your consultations.
They're quite aware of what they're going through…

The quote explodes in shards of glass and the camera focuses on a public high school, all concrete with a few glass panes, a prime example of Stalin-esque architecture in America. A clock reads 6:56 AM, and a variety of camera shots reveal a school of straight lines, littered and graffitied. Each of the five students appears at the school, just before 7, with parents somewhat frazzled, bemused, or detached. Only the stoner arrives without parental escort.

The vice principal arrives in mock *Dirty Harry* fashion. "It is now 7:06 and you have exactly 8 hours and 54 minutes to think about why you are here, to ponder the error of your ways."

From the opening moments, things fall apart for the administrator. "Yeah, I've got a question. Does Barry Manilow know that you raid his wardrobe?" the stoner asks. After a morning of adversity among the students and rather realistic sexuality, a certain harmony begins to prevail in the afternoon, especially as the students begin to sacrifice for each other.

Whatever its faults, Hughes' movie offers the most realistic story about the youth of my generation and coming of age in the mid-1980s.

Dear Mr. Vernon, we accept the fact that we had to sacrifice a whole Saturday in detention for whatever it was we did wrong. But we think you're crazy to make us write an essay telling you who we think we are. You see us as you want to see us. In the simplest terms and the most convenient definitions. But what we found out is that each one of us is a brain, an athlete, a basket case, a princess, and a criminal. Sincerely yours, The Breakfast Club.

Trust No One: *The X-Files*

Aliens, Neanderthals, poltergeists, more aliens, bumbling bureau-crats, cabals, still more aliens, pyrokinetics, artificial intelligence, religious cults, were-creatures, eugenicists, mutants, stoners, more bumbling and malicious bureaucrats, and a few more aliens. Quite a motley crew of characters. Then, after each teaser, the smeared and ghostly credits played, usually with a final thump and the statement: "The Truth Is Out There." Every once in a while, though, variations would surprise us, such as "Trust No One," "Resist or Serve," "Every-thing Dies," and "Apology Is Policy." These various creatures, these possibilities, these seductions, and these impossibilities haunted our Friday night screens back in 1993, in a show that revolutionized everything from entertainment to libertarian paranoia. Admittedly, some of season one seems dated in hindsight, but there's a reason the *X-Files* mattered so much when it first arrived on our television sets over three decades ago and why the series remains relevant (and alive) to this day.

Created by Chris Carter (a native Californian who had worked for Disney in the 1980s) and aired on the then relatively new national station Fox (one of its two main characters—in a not-so-subtle nod to Murdoch's rising empire—even has "Fox" as his unlikely first name), the *X-Files* offered intelligent pulp for the right-thinking person. The camera angles, the cinematography, and the lighting resembled the big screen more than the small, no matter how limited the special effects budget. The lighting was extraordi-narily creepy, made even creepier by Mark Snow's haunting soundtrack of atmospheric electronica. Carter, an excellent script writer, also hired a number of the best writers and directors at the time, including David Nutter, James Wong, and Glen Morgan. The show lasted a full nine seasons (1993–2002), two theatrical releases (1998 and 2008), several best-selling novels (by Kevin J. Anderson and Charles Grant), and two rock albums (that is, inspired by the *X-Files*) before going into a hiatus, only to be revived, Netflix-style, over two years on Fox.

Aside from *Star Trek* and, perhaps, *Breaking Bad*, it would be difficult to find a series that has had a greater influence on American culture over the last half-century. Not only have the characters and stories become an ingrained part of American folklore and folkways, but most modern entertainment—in all of its various forms—owes something to Chris Carter's *X-Files*. Some of its influences have been obvious—such as *Fringe* and *Stranger Things*—while others, such as *Battlestar Galactica* and *Salem*, have offered more subtle nods. One of America's foremost scholars of Shakespeare, the brilliant Paul Cantor (RIP), has even written extensively and intelligently on the show, its symbolism, and its significance.

The *X-Files*, of course, did not emerge out of a vacuum. In terms of American culture and imagination, it followed in the line of Poe and Hawthorne, Bradbury and Lovecraft, O'Connor and Percy, and Serling and King. It also followed almost three decades of American interest in the occult, UFOs, and hauntings. Even figures we incorrectly remember as staid—such as the founder of post-war conservatism, Russell Kirk—gave considerable attention to all of these irrationalities in their various books and articles of the period. Interest had become so intense in UFOs during the late 1940s and 1950s (after the supposed Roswell alien crash landing of 1947) that the FBI had responded with its own form of "Internal Affairs" for the supernatural and alien, Project Blue Book. The program ended in 1970, after citizen's groups such as NICAP claimed it to be fraudulent, existing for the sake of coverup and to protect the interests of the federal government and the armed forces, not the American citizen.

And, most critically, like all good horror and science fiction, the *X-Files* played upon—and at times exacerbated—our deepest fears as a people. This is not to suggest that the *X-Files* would have failed at a different time in our history, but it certainly did not hurt that libertarian angst over Gulf 1, Ruby Ridge, and Waco, the general conservative distrust of the New World Order, and the rise of popular and consumerist radio talk shows coincided with the success of the *X-Files*. And, though Watergate was two decades over by the time the series began, Nixon's specter of corruption hangs over the entirety of season one.

The main character of the *X-Files*, Fox "Spooky" Mulder (David Duchovny), reflected the paranoid curiosity of every intelligent and liberty-minded American in the post-Cold War era, wondering just what the heck was going on in an age that rapidly and horribly left Ronald Reagan behind, even while claiming to speak in his name. Dr. Dana Scully, Mulder's skeptical and Watson-esque sidekick, reflected our more rational and patriotic side, the side that still wanted our government to be our ally, not our master. At first, Scully—through certainly attractive—is somewhat bland as a character, merely a foil to the witty Mulder. As the first season progresses, though, Gillian Anderson brings much depth to her character, especially in reference to Scully's Roman Catholicism. Naturally, the issue of faith as opposed to reason appears frequently in the series. In the pilot—which takes place a year before the series—the FBI had assigned Scully to the X-Files, hoping that the seemingly puritanical and rational Scully would debunk Mulder.

In the first season, we see a number of their bosses come and go. Some are ambitious. Some are blindly patriotic. Some are even well-meaning and well-intentioned. All, however, are so arrogant as to be unable to see beyond their own agendas, whether for the private good or the greater good. Only Mulder fully loves the common good in the first season, with Scully defiantly loyal to the person of Mulder but not to his ideas or instincts. Mulder, wounded at almost every level beyond the intellect, remembers his younger sister's disappearance when the two were just children, and is convinced his sister had been abducted by aliens. Obsessed with the loss, he then makes a name for himself as an expert on the psychotic behavior of serial killers. With his reputation in the FBI made, Mulder takes over the neglected division of the Bureau, the X-Files, which, it seems from oblique references in the show, are even older than the FBI itself.

In what would be a running gag in any other show, but seemed plausible in this one, Mulder almost always sees what he wants to see—that which is mysterious and gnostic—while Scully almost always misses everything that is not purely rational, except when it deals with faith and Catholicism. In a nod to its audience (not typical, given the pandering of the day in most Hollywood movies and shows, with the ridiculous and mocking one-liners), Scully and Mulder were both well-educated, each with advanced degrees, and each prone to speak in complicated sentences with actual and meaningful vocabulary and grammar. Never did they speak down to the audience, though exposition could be long, at times, depending upon the success or not of the individual writers.

Vitally, Mulder is the one person who always stands for truth, no matter the cost to himself or his reputation. A crusader to his core, Mulder never backs down. At one critical moment in season one, as the FBI is hoping to shut down the X-Files, Mulder fiercely challenges the committee trying to crucify him: "No one, no government agency, has jurisdiction over the truth." It's the kind of thing that made my soul soar at age 25. Now in my mid 50s, it still does.

In almost every way, the show understood the nuances of the post-Cold War world better than the so-called intellectuals and neoconservatives of that era who believed in the "End of History." The *X-Files* was not concerned with the end of history, but with the threatened annihilation of what was (and is permanently) human. The show, though cheesy at times, dealt seriously with the corruption of the republic, the militarization of the police, and the rise of empire abroad.

For a variety of reasons, I stopped watching television shows (other than news) around 1981, when I was in seventh grade. I never stopped going to the cinema and watching classic movies, but television in the 1980s did nothing for me. I was far more interested in exploring my local environs, reading, and writing. For whatever reason, I happened to see the pilot of the *X-Files* on its first appearance. I had just turned 25. A friend taped the shows for me (God bless him!), and I finally bought my first TV in 1996, wanting to watch both *X-Files* and *Babylon 5*. As I look back on 1993, while I was working on my PhD, the *X-Files* seems as important to informing my worldview as were the many hours I spent reading *Liberty*, *Reason*, *National Review*, *Chronicles*, and *The Freeman*.

Re-watching the series now with my children reminds me just how critical the decade of the 1990s was. Though it probed into the most difficult issues of society, conformity, individuality, empire, and humanity, the *X-Files* exists in a more innocent era, a pre-9-11 era that still believed a national security state to be but one possible future, not the nightmare dystopia it has become. At least, not with certainty. Ronald Reagan gave us breathing room, economically and globally. We lived on the capital of the former until 2008, but we blew the global stability within two years of Reagan leaving the White House. Equally, Chris Carter's *X-Files* gave us a warning not only about creeping empire and the New World Order, but about the dangers of an intrusive security state, claiming to exist in the name of its people, but retarding the free will of those same people at every turn. Carter's warning was a massive and brilliant one. For the most part, we ignored it, and we suffer for it, immensely. When it comes to governments, corporations, and colossal entities, I agree with Carter, Mulder, and Scully: Trust no one.

Batman on Film, Part I
Bruce Timm's Animated Series

On September 5, 1992, a very young Bruce Timm aired the first episode of what would become an expansive universe, now known simply as the DCAU, the Detective Comics Animated Universe.

The story that appeared on that first day, "On Leather Wings," was written by Mitch Brian, who, amazingly enough, graduated six years ahead of me from the same high school in central Kansas and had already become a legend because of his writing skills. Given the relatively young age of all involved in its production and the fact that television animation was regarded—properly so—as third-rate muck, written to sell toys to bored middle-class kids, *Batman: The Animated Series* is nothing less than a profound statement of art and intensity over crassness and commercialism.

With the success of the first two Tim Burton live-action Batman movies, *Batman* (1989) and *Batman Returns* (1992), Warner Brothers wanted to capitalize on the property. Would it be possible to introduce Batman to a whole new generation of fans? Timm, a self-taught cartoonist and animator who had paid his dues on other kid shows while in his twenties—some good, some not—agreed to do it, but only if he could do it well. He liked the Burton movies, but he did not want to copy them, and he did not want his cartoon to be as gritty. As dark, sure; but not as gritty. He also wanted to get back to Batman's pulp origins, as a masked detective and vigilante, a master crime solver and quasi-anarchist.

Timm assembled a powerful team—not just Mitch Brian (who wrote four episodes total), but other excellent writers such as Paul Dini and Alan Burnett. Others, such as Denny O'Neil, Gerry Conway, Michael Reaves, Marv Wolfman, Len Wein, Michael Barr, and Elliot Maggin, also wrote for the series.

Timm also wisely and critically chose Eric Radomski as production designer and co-producer. Wanting to design a Gotham that was dark and sleek rather than dark and gritty, they did something revolutionary; they painted their stories on black paper. No one had done this before, as animation was expected to be bright and buoyant. The backgrounds, in fact, were so black that Timm and Radomski feared they would not pass FCC guidelines, and they also worried that the technology of the average home television set at the time might not reveal all they wanted to express with the setting. They also took from the real-life art deco architectural designs of men such as Hugh Ferriss from the 1920s, and they relied fundamentally on light—when it rarely appeared—to set mood and tone.

With the Batman stories mostly set during twilight, evening, and night, the incorporation of real art deco architecture and the use of black paper resulted in some of the most stunning art—"dark deco" as it's now known—to appear on television. The one downside to all of this—which the Timm team still regrets—is that dust of any kind shows like snow on the black paper copies, thus making them difficult to transfer to Blu-ray. Frankly, from a viewer's standpoint, this "dust-snow" doesn't bother me at all—there's a quality to it akin to the scratch and pop of the needle on vinyl. It's comforting, not off-putting. The few flaws only make the great art even greater.

Given the "dark deco" of the series, it's never clear exactly when *Batman: The Animated Series* takes place. Measured by the buildings and the cars, it's sometime in the 1940s. Yet, several phones and computers suggest the 1990s. Clothing styles are generally late 1940s. The timelessness only adds to the noir mystique of the show.

Two other elements make the show timeless. First, Warner Brothers allowed Timm and Radomski to hire the voice talent necessary to make a great show. To this day, many Batman fans instantly recognize Kevin Conroy (RIP) as the Batman and Mark Hamill as the Joker. Other great actors from the time provided voiceovers for the series: Efrem Zimbalist, Bob Hastings, Roddy McDowell, Michael Ansara, David Warner, Ron Perlman, Adrienne Barbeau, Ed Asner, Kate Mulgrew, Michael York, Paul Williams, Loren Lester, Robert Costanzo, Melissa Gilbert, Brock Peters, Diana Muldaur, and Julie Brown. Quite an impressive list, all assembled by Andrea Romano, under Timm and Radomski's oversight.

Second, Warner Brothers allowed Timm and Radomski to hire Shirley Walker and her full orchestra to write all original symphonic music for each episode. The music was so popular at the time—

some of the best classical being written in the early 1990s—that one can still purchase compilations of the music in a variety of volumes and from at least two different companies, competing with one another.

It's well worth remembering that Bruce Timm and co. were revolutionizing animation for television in the way that Disney was, at the same time, on the big screen. Much of what Timm introduced in 1992 we now take for granted. But when he and his team did it in 1992, it seemed wildly eccentric to the industry. Pixar didn't exist yet, and television was still limited to just a few channels, making airtime extremely precious. Timm and Radomski refused to compromise their vision, and a far-sighted studio exec let them get away with it. Looking back on how fierce Timm had to be with shoddy writers and shoddy artwork, he's now embarrassed by how nasty he could be (or had to be), but, frankly, it was worth it. Timm's integrity really shows, even twenty-five years later.

And, of course, all the production values in the world mean nothing if the stories don't amount to much. Thankfully, Timm and Radomski's vision included some of the best stories ever written for television. While every American knows the story of Bruce Wayne and Batman, Timm and Radomski made his story fresh, focusing on his detective skills but also on his double life—as billionaire businessman and as vigilante. The pain of sleepless nights and constant brawls wears on Wayne, and Robin (now in college) and Alfred the Butler must manage Wayne's moods and darker impulses. In short, they have to temper him, preventing him from becoming the very thing he abhors. Indeed, the show loved to play with the ideas of duality and the darkness of staring too long into the abyss.

The sixth episode, "It's Never Too Late," for example, explores both major themes as two brothers near the end of their lives. Best friends as children, they had gone radically different ways, with one becoming a Catholic priest and the other a crime boss. Rather than confront the crime boss directly, Batman allows the priest brother to remind him of good, evil, and choice. If there's the possibility of redemption for a mobster, there's such for anyone.

Eighty-five episodes made up the original series, with several movies as well as variations and television spinoffs between 1992 and 2006: *Superman*; *Batman Beyond*; *Justice League*; *Zeta Project*; and *Static Shock*. Characters now considered "mainstream" in the DC universe, such as Harley Quinn and Renee Montoya, were created for Timm's *Batman: The Animated Series*.

Of the movies that came out of *Batman: The Animated Series*, the best, by far, is *The Mask of the Phantasm*. Originally meant to be a direct-to-video release, it so impressed the studio that it allowed it an opening in movie theaters, nationwide, back in 1993. Shocked by the change of mind by the studio, Timm and Radomski had to revise the movie—especially its format—very quickly. The result, however, is stunning. Not only is it a great Batman movie—certainly the greatest made up through 1993—it is a great movie about free will's complications and progress's deceptions.

Given the power of film, Batman is a critical marker for modern western civilization. Batman is our urban American mythological symbol, equivalent to the frontier literary characters Natty Bumppo and Huck Finn. When culture mocks Batman, as the leftists of the 1960s did with the character in the horrible campy sitcom of that decade, or Tim Burton did in a bizarre carnival-esque way with his *Batman* and *Batman Returns* during the Reagan-Bush years, it is a strong indication that we have fundamentally lost our way as a people.

As a western hero—in the line of Aeneas—Batman must seek order in a world of chaos. He must trust to natural law when positive law has gone astray. He must, no matter the cost, protect the innocent from those who would manipulate the things (and persons) of this world for their own gain.

Most importantly, as Timm and Radomski so successfully demonstrated in their magisterial run of Batman and his allies, virtue matters more than anything else in this fallen world, whether it's in creating a work of art or using that work of art to tell a story.

Batman on Film, Part II
Christopher Nolan's Dark Knight Trilogy

> "I see a beautiful city and a brilliant people rising from this abyss. I see the lives for which I lay down my life, peaceful, useful, prosperous and happy. I see that I hold a sanctuary in their hearts, and in the hearts of their descendants, generations hence. It is a far, far better thing that I do, than I have ever done; it is a far, far better rest that I go to than I have ever known."—Obituary for Bruce Wayne, taken from Dickens's *A Tale of Two Cities*

In 2005, Time Warner released *Batman Begins*, the first high-budget film by Anglo-American filmmaker Christopher Nolan (*Dunkirk*, *Inception*, *Interstellar*), known at the time only to a few cinema nuts for his low-budget but intensely artful and intellectual films. The Batman franchise—from novels to comic books to movies to toys—had been a huge property in terms of profit for Time Warner for years. Still, no matter what, most Americans thought of Batman as a really neat comic book figure. "Be yourself. Unless you can be Batman. Then, be Batman." When the character appeared on screens, he had done so as a counter-cultural buffoon in the late 1960s, and as a gothic and carnival-esque weirdo in the hands of Tim Burton and his followers, two decades later. Only Bruce Timm's excellent animated Batman series, aired in the afternoons during the early 1990s, did the character justice, but, because of the medium, it reached only a small handful of diehard Batman fans. Could Nolan transfer his intensity and intellectualism in film to Batman, thus transforming him from a pop sensation into a cultural mainstay, giving the property gravitas and the studio profit?

Nolan, his wife, Emma, and his brother Jonah served as the core development team of his films, but he also often employed a troupe of actors, including Christian Bale and Cillian Murphy. The entire group was interested, but Nolan, though a long-time Batman fan, did not know the comics. He had never been a collector or a reader in the comic book field, and to make a proper Batman film, he needed an expert. Wisely, he turned to David Goyer, a native of

Detroit and a life-long comic book fan and writer. Goyer had not only written for DC and Marvel (the two main comic book companies and friendly rivals), but he had also written some extraordinary film scripts, such as the Gothic noir dystopia *Dark City* (1998), arguably one of most imaginative science fiction films ever made.

In part because he was untried and in part because of his own artistic sensibilities, Nolan decided to make *Batman Begins* as a stand-alone movie. He had no plan at the time for making a sequel, believing this would diminish his own effectiveness as a filmmaker. Simply put, he wanted every member of his team to see this film as a one-time opportunity, holding nothing back in its making.

> People ask if we'd always planned a trilogy. This is like being asked whether you had planned on growing up, getting married, having kids. The answer is complicated. When David and I first started cracking open Bruce's story, we flirted with what might come after, then backed away, not wanting to look too deep into the future. I didn't want to know everything that Bruce couldn't; I wanted to live with him. I told David and Jonah to put everything they knew into each film as we made it. The entire cast and crew put all they had into the first film. Nothing held back. Nothing saved for next time.

As Nolan approached the story, he decided two critical things. First, he wanted the film to be as realistic as possible. If something happened that could not be explained rationally, he excised even the idea of it from the film. Everything from the Batmobile to the reaction of the police had to be utterly realistic. This film would be set in the real world, not in a fantasy world of aliens, magic, and super-powered beings. If the Batman headgear needed two ears, for example, there needed to be an explanation for those two ears. If Batman jumped from building to building, as another example, there needed to be a reason why and explanation as to how.

Second, Nolan approached the character not as a comic-book superhero, but as a western legend, a myth, larger than any single person, event, or even culture. Nolan was tapping into something already in the Batman mythos but not explicitly understood by the larger public. Just like Natty Bumppo of James Fenimore Cooper's *Leatherstocking Tales* and Huck Finn of Mark Twain's two books dealing with the same, Bruce Wayne/Batman stands as a crucial American symbol. If Bumppo and Finn personify the American frontier of the 19th century, so Bruce Wayne/Batman is the great mythological figure of 20th- and 21st-century urban America. Named after the revolutionary and Washingtonian general Mad Anthony Wayne, coming from one of the wealthiest of American families, and, as a family, the builders and defenders of Gotham City, a Platonic shadow of New York, populated by 30 million people, Bruce Wayne believes it his aristocratic duty to protect the poor and oppressed from the wealthy and the corrupt. He is an Arthurian—but also deeply American—figure.

Brilliantly, Nolan wrapped the entire Dark Knight trilogy into the significance of myth, and the significance of myth into the story. When attempting to explain to Alfred, his father-figure, butler, and accomplice, what he hopes to do when returning to Gotham City, Wayne says: "People need dramatic examples to shame them out of apathy. I can't do this as Bruce Wayne. A man is just flesh and blood, and can be ignored or destroyed. But a symbol . . . as a symbol I can be incorruptible, everlasting."

Several themes inform each movie. The first movie deals with justice and fear. The second with free will and anarchy. The third with hope and reformation.

In Nolan's typical but eccentric way, the first movie jumps repeatedly in time, creating a whole out of the non-linear. The story is a familiar one, at least to Americans born after 1939. Nolan retells the traditional story, but he adds his own tastes and vision.

The son of the wealthiest couple in the greatest city of the western world, Gotham, Bruce Wayne stands as a young boy with his parents in "Crime Alley," having left the opera early. There, a killer takes their money and jewels, shooting both of Bruce's parents. Left an orphan, Bruce is raised by the family butler, Alfred Pennyworth. After dropping out of Princeton and ineffectively confronting the man he believes ordered the hit on his parents, Wayne departs Gotham City for years, traveling throughout the world, learning what it means to fight, to suffer, and to survive. The purpose, as he sees it, is to hone every skill he possesses—physical as well as intellectual—to return to Gotham to protect the innocent.

In *Batman Begins*, Wayne finds himself in a high Tibetan temple belonging to an evil and inverted type of Knights Templar, the "League of Shadows," an organization that demands the end of corruption of public officials, calling them to account by destroying any city that has become unrepentantly corrupt. They claim responsibility for having destroyed Rome, Constantinople, and London, across the centuries. Now, they openly admit, they need to take out Gotham. Tellingly, the leader is a man named Ra's Al Ghul, an Arabic title meaning "Head of the Demon." The League claims itself superior to all political organizations in promoting what it sees as justice, a harmony derived from a very Nietzschean desire for the "will to act." The League of Shadows, Ra's Al Ghul explains, "has been a check against human corruption for thousands of years. We sacked Rome. Loaded trade ships with plague rats. Burned London to the ground. Every time a civilization reaches the pinnacle of its decadence, we return to restore the balance."

Though trained by the League of Shadows to be the heir to Ra's Al Ghul, Wayne rejects their philosophy, destroys their temple, and returns to Gotham, presuming the League to have come to its end.

Back in Gotham, he assumes the primal symbol of his own fears, a bat, hoping to employ terror against evil. As the Batman, he stands as a living gargoyle, adorning the cathedral of western civilization while driving away rival evils. In his fight, he relies on four persons to sustain him: Alfred, to serve as Watson to his Holmes; Police Lieutenant Jim Gordon, the only honest cop in Gotham; Lucius Fox, a master engineer and entrepreneur; and Rachel Dawes, the one true love of his life, now an assistant district attorney. Rachel, more than anyone else, complicates Wayne's life, as she is unsure of his sanity and his intentions, especially in his assumption of the Bat persona.

The movie—operatic in a Wagnerian way from opening to final scene—concludes with Wayne barely defeating the revived Ra's Al Ghul and his League of Shadows, not as dead or wounded as Wayne had presumed. In the war against the League of Shadows, Wayne Manor is destroyed, Rachel admits that she cannot love a man who fights crime as a bat, and a poison is loosed upon an area of Gotham known as "The Narrows," a decayed part of the city that houses the poor and the insane. What the consequences of the latter are remain unknown at the end of the movie, but Gordon, now fully in alliance with the Batman, shows him the "calling card" of a new masked criminal, a grimy playing card of a joker.

The second movie, *The Dark Knight* (2008), begins with the Joker and his henchmen stealing from a mob bank. The heist, filmed as a tribute to such neo-noir crime classics as *The French Connection* (1971) and *Heat* (1995), goes off as planned, introducing the audience to the face of diabolic anarchy and insanity, Heath Ledger's stunning Joker. Ledger, tragically, threw himself so much into the role of insanity that he committed suicide shortly after filming the movie and a full six months before the film's release. Not only a personal tragedy, his suicide proved a huge blow to Nolan and crew.

Unlike the first movie, filmed almost entirely in shadow and with a gothic noir aesthetic, based on vertical lines, *The Dark Knight* presents a shiny and sunny Gotham, its architectural lines straight, sleek, clean, and horizontal. Unlike the first or third movie, the story—atypically for Nolan—is linear, driving relentlessly from the opening heist to the final tragic moments for all involved.

The story revolves around the Joker's attempt to destroy Gotham from within, introducing anarchy, as he claims.

> I'm a dog chasing cars... I wouldn't know what to do with one if I caught it. I just do things. I'm just the wrench in the gears. I hate plans. Yours, theirs, everyone's. Maroni has plans. Gordon has plans. Schemers trying to control their worlds. I'm not a schemer, I show the schemers how pathetic their attempts to control things really are. So when I say that you and your girlfriend was nothing personal, you know I'm telling the truth.

Whatever the Joker might claim about anarchy and being the antithesis of a planner, he is a master chessman, planning and scheming, always three or four moves ahead of those around him. According to all law enforcement databases, the Joker should not exist. He has no prints on record, he's clearly trained in some form of special ops, and even his clothing is all custom-made.

In addition to the theme of anarchy and plans, the movie deals with free will and duality. If we choose A, are we doomed to follow B? If we follow B, have we destroyed all future options? Most importantly, the question manifests itself in the personal story of Harvey Dent, a young and courageous district attorney, ready to become Gotham's White Knight, replacing Batman's Dark Knight as the face of decency in the city.

To prove that no real goodness resides in the world, the Joker plays upon Dent's weaknesses, killing his girlfriend (Rachel Dawes; also Wayne's one love) and driving him to madness. In the final scene, with Gotham not knowing that Dent has fallen to evil, Dent takes Gordon's family hostage. In the fight to protect Gordon's children, Batman and Dent plunge over a building ledge, with Dent dying. Batman tells Gordon that he will take the blame, though he has done nothing wrong. The movie ends with Batman having saved hundreds of lives, defeating the Joker and Dent, but now becoming a hunted man, vilified as a murderer. "You'll hunt me. You'll condemn me. You'll set the dogs on me." As the film ends, Gordon explains to his son that Batman is "a silent guardian, a watchful protector, a dark knight."

Once again, Nolan had no intention of making a third movie. The death of his friend Heath Ledger especially rattled him, and he was not ready to go back into the world of Batman. Still, he claims, the Batman would not leave him alone, and he had to write the third movie to find out exactly how the story turned out.

The final movie of the trilogy, *The Dark Knight Rises*, is not only the best of the trilogy, it is, arguably, one of the finest movies ever made, a true achievement of the cinematic arts, certainly a movie worthy of Alfred Hitchcock or John Ford. It is also, perhaps, the single most important defense of western civilization ever to reach a Hollywood screen. That the cultural left did not rip it to shreds proves that they either did not watch it or simply did not understand it.

Inspired by Charles Dickens's *A Tale of Two Cities*, though much of the dialogue might have been written by the grand Anglo-Irish statesman Edmund Burke, Nolan's *The Dark Knight Rises* is a retelling of the events of the French Revolution in Paris. In place of

Robespierre is a mercenary, chemically enhanced, from either Eastern Europe or the Middle East, known only as Bane. Bane, it must be noted, is the creation of noted writer Chuck Dixon, a man both admired and reviled in the comic book world for his conservatism. Working with several of Wayne's competitors in business, Bane has spent six months rebuilding the infrastructure of Gotham City, secretly lacing all of the concrete in streets, bridges, tunnels, and sewers with explosives.

Coming out of retirement at age 43, the Batman investigates, but when he encounters Bane in the sewers, Bane ably defeats him, breaking his back. Claiming to be the fulfillment of the League of Shadows, Bane takes the broken Wayne to a prison somewhere in the Middle East (in actuality, an ancient city on the Pakistan-Indian border) and leaves him there to die. With a broken back in this hellhole, the only thing Wayne can do is watch a TV set to a Gotham City channel. As a part of his punishment, Bane wants Wayne to see the fall of Gotham as it implodes, collapsing in on itself from the weight of its own corruption. In lines that could have been lifted straight out of volume I of Alexander Solzhenitsyn's *The Gulag*, Bane explains to Wayne that while he is happy to have broken Wayne's body, the prison is meant to destroy his soul.

Upon his return to Gotham, Bane lets loose all of the explosives, destroying the city's infrastructure as well as access to and from the main island—the equivalent of Manhattan. In his takeover of the city, he warns the United States not to intervene, as he wields a nuclear weapon with a six-mile blast radius. Should the U.S. intervene, Bane promises to detonate the bomb, killing all on the island. He has, thus, separated Gotham from the U.S., creating his own city-state. In the newly-conquered city of Gotham, Bane frees all of the prisoners of Blackgate Prison (the Bastille) and declares the city to be under the control of "the people." The people, Bane says truthfully, have been deceived by the leadership of Gotham. Harvey Dent was not the White Knight, but an insane criminal and murderer. Thus, all of Gotham's successes over the eight years since Dent's death have been nothing but a lie.

> We take Gotham from the corrupt. The rich. The oppressors of generations who've kept you down with the myth of opportunity. And, we give it to you, the people. Gotham is yours. None shall interfere. Do as you please.... For an army will be raised. The powerful will be ripped from their decadent nests, and cast into the cold world the rest of us have known and endured. Courts will be convened. The spoils will be enjoyed. Blood will be shed.

In Soviet style, the criminal, the insane, and the poor ravage the homes, property, and persons of the wealthy, inverting the entire socio-economic structure of Gotham. The people—under the judgeship of Dr. Jonathan Crane, the "Scarecrow" and creator of the poisons of the first film—establish courts to sentence the wealthy for having preyed upon the poor. All such trials end in the execution of the guilty. Nothing like this level of anti-communism had been seen in Hollywood since Roland Joffé's revealing if horrifying look into Cambodia under the Khmer Rouge, 1984's *The Killing Fields*.

In the Middle Eastern prison, Bruce Wayne heals and regains his strength, spiritually as well as physically, climbing out of the pit (Plato's Cave), liberating himself and his fellow prisoners. Wayne knows that only one person had ever escaped the prison before. This inspires him.

Returning to Gotham City, Wayne as Batman takes control of the remaining police under Gordon's command, raising a counter-revolutionary army. Leading hundreds of police into battle, he and his greatest ally, a somewhat reformed jewel thief by the name of Selina Kyle, battle Bane and his revolutionaries. In hand-to-hand combat outside the Gotham City stock exchange, Kyle and Batman barely defeat Bane. Still, there remains the nuclear bomb. Taking his Bat—a hover aircraft based on the Harrier and the Blackhawk—Batman flies the bomb out of the city, over the Atlantic, and lets it detonate safely. Everyone, however, presumes that Batman has died as well.

At the funeral—attended only by four loved ones—a shell-shocked Gordon, who has only now come to realize the true identity of the Batman, reads from *A Tale of Two Cities*. Looking at the grave of Wayne, next to that of Wayne's mother and father, Alfred breaks down, believing that his entire life has been a failure. He had wanted to serve the Waynes, but he had overseen the death of the entire family.

The movie ends with Wayne Manor becoming a home for orphaned boys, St. Swithin's, led by a Catholic priest, with Lucius Fox realizing that Wayne might have survived the flight over the Atlantic, with Gordon refurbishing the long-disused Bat signal, and with Alfred sitting in an outside café in France, seeing Bruce and Selina sitting together, in love, at a neighboring table.

Western civilization has survived, but only barely, and only with incredible sacrifice at every level. "I see that I hold a sanctuary in their hearts, and in the hearts of their descendants, generations hence," Dickens had written.

While some might still see merely a children's comic-book super-hero made glittery with a Hollywood budget in the Dark Knight trilogy, it would be impossible not to recognize Nolan's pure genius, if one takes an objective (or, at least, somewhat objective) view-point. Unlike, say, Peter Jackson, who dumbed down *The Lord of the Rings*, Christopher Nolan leavened Batman. Tolkien was made less by Jackson, but Batman was made more by Nolan.

In Nolan's expert hands, Batman becomes what he always meant to be: an American Odysseus, an American Aeneas, an American Arthur, an American Beowulf, and an American Thomas More. He serves as what Eric Voegelin would have identified as an anamnesis, a symbolic means by which we return to first principles. Batman resonates with us because he is the best of us and the best of what came before us. Bruce Wayne is the embodiment of western virtue and heroism.

Batman on Film, Part III
The Batman

The story begins on Halloween, almost exactly 20 years after the murder of Thomas and Martha Wayne. A new killer—an internet sensation, as it turns out—is on the loose, violently ridding Gotham City of its excesses. The Batman, now two years into his mission, must not only solve the mysteries behind the killings but end the killings themselves. He has a great ally in a youngish James Gordon of the Gotham City Police Department and soon also forms an alliance with a jaded bartender and cat burglar, Selina Kyle, as he uncovers the relationship of the Penguin with crime lord Carmine Falcone. Throughout the story, the Batman serves as the ultimate detective, trying to hew some kind of moral and ethical line, especially difficult as his methods and attitude creepily resemble those of the Riddler. The entire story takes place between October 31 and November 6, giving it a *Stranger Things* feel.

So much for a broad overview. Now things get personal. As a Batman geek, I wanted so badly to be enthralled by this movie. I wanted Gotham to sweep me up and immerse me in its wallowing corruption. I wanted every nook and cranny of the city to ooze with anxious anticipation. I wanted villains who cried out with unadulterated anguish, and my Batman dark, gritty, mythic, and obsessed with justice. But I also wanted a fully realized Batcave and Batmobile, a few Batarangs, a fatherly Alfred, and a virtuous Wayne family legacy.

That is, I wanted desperately to fall in love with Matt Reeves' *The Batman*. Was I asking too much?

After two viewings, I must admit, I'm only bemused by the spectacle of it all, wondering if those six hours (three per showing) will count against my already steep debt in purgatory.

There *were* things to love about the movie, I'll admit. The acting—especially by Robert Pattinson as the Batman, Paul Dano as the Riddler, and Colin Farrell as the Penguin—was superb. That by

John Turturro as Carmine Falcone, Zoe Kravitz as Selina Kyle, and Andy Serkis as Alfred, less so, sadly. Often, these latter three seemed stiff and merely going through the motions.

I also deeply appreciated that Reeves and the other creators took the comics very seriously, relying upon *The Long Halloween, Year One, When in Rome, Hush, Gotham by Gaslight* (the suit!), and *No Man's Land* as obvious inspirations.

Gotham, to be sure, feels like Gotham. It's not New York or Newark or Chicago. It's a metropolis all its own, complete with all the nuances of Gotham. For example, the film references specific areas of Gotham detailed in the comics and also ties together the Waynes and the Arkhams as old and leading families of the city.

But there were as many, if not more, head-scratchers as there were accomplishments in the movie. I'll offer just seven.

First, at the film's start, Bruce Wayne offers a voiceover that suits the film noir mood beautifully. "Two years in, and I'm a nocturnal animal... the Bat-Signal is not just a call, but a warning... Fear is a tool... I am the shadows... I'm vengeance... The city is eating itself. Maybe beyond saving, but I have to try to push myself." It was chilling and excellent. The voiceover ends, however, minutes into the movie and doesn't return until the conclusion, and then only to state something about the Batman being about hope rather than about vengeance.

Second, about two-thirds into the film, Alfred simply disappears, his last scene capturing a quick reconciliation with Bruce over a bizarre matter, the camera lingering on the two holding hands.

Third, the theme music for the Riddler is Franz Schubert's "Ave Maria." Seriously. Every time the psychopathic Riddler does something mischievous (and, truth be told, downright evil), the "Ave Maria" plays. Frankly, it's diabolic. For some reason, the Batman's theme (at least at the beginning and end of the movie) is Nirvana's "Something in the Way."

Fourth, even though Gotham's political, social, and economic structures are totally corrupt, the mayor elected in the movie—Bella Reál (Jayme Lawson)—suddenly demonstrates moxie, dedication, and downright bravado. It would've been far more appropriate to the themes of the story to have made her the mastermind manipulating all things behind the scenes, the devil's devil, or, at the very least, to have her as a party to the overall corruption. As it is, she seems too good to be true, especially given the tone of the movie.

Fifth, Batman's relationship with the police and first responders is schizophrenic, to say the least. In some scenes, he's allowed access to a criminal investigation, working alongside the GCPD, but in others he's a wanted fugitive, fighting his way through hordes of cops. As a movie, *The Batman* never makes clear what the true relationship is between the Caped Crusader and the Gotham authorities, weakening the overall atmosphere and plot. Indeed, the Batman's relationship with the police changes so swiftly in the movie that you're tempted to throw your hands up in sheer frustration. Is today the day he works with the police? Or is today the day in which the police attack him as an interfering vigilante? James Gordon, thankfully, remains a firm ally throughout the movie at least.

Sixth, this Batman (unlike, say, that of Zach Snyder) disdains the use of guns and seems to have a "no kill" rule, which has been the norm for Batman since the early 1940s. However, given the stunning brutality of the Penguin/Batmobile chase, it's clear that Reeves's Batman is totally fine with innumerable highway deaths.

Seven, and this one is surely personal, I despised the fact that Thomas Wayne was made out to be less than utterly virtuous. It's been the fashion of the comics (and the novels) over the past decade to question Thomas' motivations, but it has always struck me as essential to the character of Bruce Wayne that he live up to his father's fine, aristocratic, and untarnished example.

There is some unfortunate dialogue regarding Wayne's family as well. While not knowing that Bruce Wayne is the Batman, Selina Kyle, in a confessional moment, dismisses those murdered thus far (including Thomas Wayne from 20 years earlier) as "white privileged a—holes." Further, when the Batman makes a totally appropriate response about ethics, choice, and morality, Selina replies, "Choices? Whoever you are, you had to grow up rich," implying the poor have no choice but to bend or break the law.

Again, there are things to love and appreciate about this version of *The Batman*, but they are far and few between, riddled with the strange things just listed. This version of Batman is, at best, a shadow of Christopher Nolan's *The Dark Knight*. If you really need to fall in love with Batman, Nolan's version is the best. But I would also recommend Bruce Timm's *Mask of the Phantasm* or any of his animated Batman series, as well as the most recent DC Animated films, such as *Under the Red Hood* or *The Long Halloween*. There you will find captured the true spirit of the Caped Crusader.

Zach Snyder's *Man of Steel*

In one of the best comic-book stories of the last several generations, Frank Miller's *The Dark Knight Returns* (1986), Batman confronts Superman. Years into a dystopian future in which the United
States has become more-or-less imperialist, fundamentalist, and
oppressive, the conservative and patriotic Superman has rather
unthinkingly joined forces with America to maintain order. Batman, true to form, has created a libertarian resistance, opposing all
repression with vigilante ferocity. Superman, he knows, must be
taken down before the grip of the government's control can be broken.

In *The Man of Steel*, writers David Goyer and Christopher Nolan
create a dystopia of Superman's (Kal-el's) home planet, Krypton,
more ordered but as fascistic as what Miller prophesied for Earth
thirty years earlier. Krypton has actually entered a post-imperialist
phase, its own reach having decayed centuries earlier as the new
home planet (the original planet is long gone) has become the over-
used playground of militaristic, rigid castes. The government has
allowed no natural births for time immemorial, with each child
coming into existence for a specifically defined purpose, ready to
serve her or his part in the greater good. This is a cold, cold Sparta,
gone mad.

Before going any further in this review, let me state that while I'm
no longer a movie buff (I used to be, long before having so many little Birzers running around the house), I do consider David Goyer
one of the finest writers of our era. His ability to mix serious existential questions with science fiction, fantasy, and myth is nothing
short of brilliant. In particular, I think his *Dark City* is one of the
best science fiction movies ever made, and his work on *The Crow*
and *Flash Forward* was excellent. His masterpiece, though, is the
2005 *Batman Begins*, a work closer to opera than traditional cinema.
Every one of his stories really focuses on the nature of existence and
the difficulties of being human, no matter whether the adversaries
are flying alien butchers (*Man of Steel*), hovering alien vampires

(*Dark City*), or psychiatric madmen (*Batman Begins*). I would go so far as to argue that Goyer is one of our best living myth-makers, an artist who knows the essence of story and that our role within existence must, in some way, conform to a transcendent justice. Goyer always presents struggle with a backdrop of pervasive, if somewhat elusive, grace.

The Plot
Recognizing the errors of their homeworld and its insular, rigid culture, Kal-el's parents not only sacrifice themselves to redeem the past, but they also do so by defying the reigning law and procreating naturally. As it turns out, their son (Kal-el) is the first natural birth in memory. They consciously want to build the future as Providence erases the past, Krypton imploding then exploding from years of abuse by its current occupants.

Surprisingly, at least to me, the destruction of Krypton and a fanatic, violent attempt to preserve the artificial order of the culture sets the stage for much of the conflict in the overall plot of the movie. When the would-be tyrant, Zod, attempts a coup and confronts his friend-turned-enemy Jor-el (Kal-el's father), he screams "heresy" when learning that Jor-el and his wife have defied the eugenic rules of their society. He kills Jor-el with the thrust of a concealed blade. Even while being tried and found guilty for his attempted coup, Zod vows to hunt down Kal-el, killing him in the name of revenge, believing such a death might help redeem the "crimes" of the parents. The surviving government sentences Zod and his accomplices to the Phantom Zone, an otherworldly, two-dimensional prison.

Immediately following the exile, Kal-el's mother comforts a robot servant and Krypton explodes. And we're only 19 minutes and 25 seconds into the movie.

The entire middle of the movie centers, non-chronologically, on Kal-el being raised by his adopted parents, Jonathan (Kevin Costner) and Martha Kent (Diane Lane), in Kansas; his very angst-ridden struggles to discover himself; and Lois Lane's hunt for him based on too many internet rumors to ignore.

Though every actor does a fine job in the movie, Costner as Pa and Lane as Ma really steal the show. The Kents love their adopted son dearly, but the father especially fears what kind of man his boy will become and what the world will think of him. His mother has faith that Clark will grow up well and do good (and well). Far more skeptical, Pa wants the family to keep to themselves as long as possible, allowing Kal-el to develop and accept his power before presenting him to a distrusting world. In a wonderfully stirring moment, Pa takes charge of an interstate of halted travelers, soon to be hit by a tornado. Saving a number of his fellow travelers, Pa chooses to die in the tornado rather than allow his son to reveal his powers too early in his life.

As the profound Christian humanist Stratford Caldecott had argued, there exist a number of parallels to the Christ story here. Ma makes a wonderful Mary, and Pa is the perfect Joseph. Kal-el, it turns out, has far more in common with Christ than not. Commentators have been noting these parallels since Superman first arrived on the cultural front in 1939, but *Man of Steel*, as Caldecott and Chris Morrissey have beautifully argued, embraces not just the forms of Christianity but the essence of the faith as well. Charity and faith abound.

Amy Adams, not surprisingly, delivers a gorgeous performance of Lois Lane. Adams had already proven her acting genius in movies as strange and diverse as *Enchanted* and *The Muppet Movie*. By no means glamorous in the modern, plastic Hollywood sense, Adams radiates wholesome integrity and true beauty. Sadly, her dialogue at the beginning of *Man of Steel* is a bit clumsy. Trying to make her tough, Goyer and Nolan make their only misstep in the entire film. They give her course and uncouth words relating to male body parts as she confronts a strong-willed male military officer. I don't want to dwell on this single flaw too long, but suffice it to say, Goyer and Nolan's dialogue comes across as an early 1990s apology written by clueless men who try to think what feminists might be thinking. Adams, being a true woman and not an artificial one, can't deliver the lines with any justice, and I visibly winced in embarrassment while getting through this—thankfully—very short scene. Let's hope a future director's cut of the movie does away with this. Adams/Lane has already proven her strength in every one of her actions, and this ridiculous dialogue does nothing to advance the film.

Though Goyer and Nolan get credit for the screenplay, much of the film's story actually comes from a well-known comic book writer, Mark Waid. In particular, *Man of Steel* borrows from *Birthright*, a reimagining of the traditional Superman story (thus, making Krypton creepy and fascistic), and from an imagined story of St. John's Revelation should superheroes and villains actually exist at the time of Apocalypse, *Kingdom Come*.

Though *Man of Steel* seems to exist in the same DC universe as *Batman Begins*, a huge gulf separates the two. In contrast to Bruce Wayne's cultured aggression and innate darkness, Kal-el is silent and unsure of himself, but, because of his devoted parents, he is certain about his morals. Wayne's Gotham City is dark and decaying, while Metropolis is bright and gleaming, and Smallville is Edenic (except for the little-kid bullies) and pastoral. While Wayne embraces punctuated violence in the name of justice, Kal-el embraces restraint in the name of love and charity. Wayne is a city kid; Kal-el is a farm boy.

In the larger DC universe, the Kents are Methodist and the Waynes are Catholic (Anglo or Roman—it's never quite certain); but the Waynes are the descendants of Arthur and bearers of the Holy Grail. In *Man of Steel*, the Kents seem to be Catholic, and at a moment of crisis, Kal-el visits a priest, seeking advice. After Clark claims to be an alien, the priest stares skeptically. As Kal-el leaves, assuming the priest has no real advice for him, the priest jumps to his feet and offers hope. It's one of the finest scenes of the movie.

Having grown up in Kansas, and having grown up with Superman (I have a nice collection of comics, dating from 1974 to 2006), I found the depictions of Kansas in the film very telling and important. Kansas serves, properly, in the film as almost all that is good, again with the exception of the childhood bullies who learn to appreciate the "weirdness" of Clark. Sadly, for those of us from Kansas, it's clear that Smallville wasn't actually filmed there. I knew from the opening shots that the fields were too lush and too flat to be Kansas. Sure enough, the farm scenes were filmed in Illinois. Still, Costner nails his role as a Stoic Kansas farmer, ready to do his duty but not ready to have his personal life or the personal life of his family known to the world. I grew up with lots and lots of Pa Kents, and I still consider them some of the most dignified men in the world.

A favorite scene for me, redeeming any flaws with filming Kansas in Illinois, arrives at the end of the movie. As a high-ranking American military officer reluctantly confronts Kal-el, asking him if he presents a national security risk, the Man of Steel answers in measured glee. "I grew up in Kansas, General. I'm about as American as it gets." While all Americans know how proud Texans are to be Texans, few know that Kansans are equally proud of being Kansans. My soul more than cheered a bit at this line.

The Virtues

Comic book characters are about the last figures in these last years of western civilization willing to practice and embody the virtues openly. The ancients (classical and Nordic) had their gods and demigods, the medievals their saints and martyrs. We moderns and postmoderns have our superheroes. After all, the differences between Heimdahl, Ignatius of Loyola, and Kal-el are matters of degree.

The entire movie *Man of Steel* honors thy mothers and fathers, prudently accepting the holy traditions of our ancestors while revealing the unholy ones to be, well, unholy. Only through the sacrifices of his two mothers and two fathers does Kal-el come to embrace his own gifts but use them not for the greater good but for the common good.

Daredevil

"Bless me, Father, for I have sinned…"

"Perhaps it would be easier if you'd tell me what you've done."

"I'm not seeking penance for what I've done, Father. I'm asking forgiveness for what I'm about to do."

Moments later, Matthew Murdock, masked in ninja attire, beats the stuffing out of an entire gang of sex slavers, freeing a number of captive women. Those are the opening few minutes of season one, episode one of Netflix's *Daredevil*. It's intense, brutal, and just.

A child left blind by an act of charity and parentless after a mob hit on his father, Matthew Murdock grows up in a Catholic orphanage in Hell's Kitchen, New York. Eventually earning a law degree at Columbia University, he eschews corporate America and employs his legal skills to aid the poor through his small-time firm, Nelson and Murdock. Franklin "Foggy" Nelson, his best friend and law partner, aspires to make something of himself (meaning get rich), but Murdock's charisma and friendship bring out his best.

True to superhero convention, Murdock did not merely lose his sight. He unwittingly traded his normal eyesight for finely honed perceptions in his four remaining senses as well as superior resistance to pain and heightened acrobatic agility. When asked if he "sees," he replies, and I'm paraphrasing, "somewhat, but as though the world is on fire." When the viewer gets a brief glimpse of what Murdock "sees," we immediately recognize a medieval vision of the angelic, the sainted, and the holy. Halos appear everywhere.

Throughout the first three seasons of the series, a number of broken people come and go. Karen Page, an aspiring journalist with all the baggage of a broken home, seems at first like a damsel in distress, but she reveals a developed sense of perseverance and intelligence beyond almost any other character in television. Foggy, though bumbling, always knows how to break the tension and bring all things back to perspective. Father Lantom, Matt's confessor, stands by Matt no matter the cost. A man's man, Lantom is a refreshingly honest priest—so rarely seen in Hollywood or on the news—who loves to drink and play pool. He's known Matt since his childhood, raising him as a son in his orphanage. He knows exactly what Murdock does at night in the back alleys of Hell's Kitchen and recognizes him for what he is—a saint and defender of the poor.

Other allies emerge when necessary. A nurse, Claire Temple (okay, that one's a bit on the nose), patches up Matt when necessary, as does a nun, Sister Maggie (Magdalene—again, some obvious Catholic symbolism). An old flame, the Asian-Greek Elektra Natchios, complicates Murdock's life with her support, sexual temptation, and heroic distraction. Murdock, for his part, would do anything to bring her to salvation, but such a commitment will exact a huge toll.

Even *Daredevil*'s main villain, Wilson Fisk (Kingpin), fascinates the viewer. Plagued by extreme emotions and control issues, Kingpin wants to dominate everything and everyone around him. His deeply intelligent and passionate evil is believable and thus utterly horrifying. He has become—at least in Hell's Kitchen—a small god, able to see the moves on the chessboard six, seven, and eight turns ahead, outwitting almost everyone around him. And those he can't outwit, he murders.

Stan Lee, Bill Everett, and Jack Kirby first created Daredevil at the beginning of the golden age of Marvel Comics in 1964. Until the late 1970s, though, he remained a second- or third-rate character, usually supporting others, especially Spider-Man. Then Frank Miller took over the art and then the writing in the late 1970s and early 1980s (and, briefly, in the early 1990s). Miller is constitutionally incapable of producing anything but absolute excellence, and his runs on the character raised Daredevil to the top tier of all Marvel and, indeed, all comic-book characters. One might readily combine the holy vengeance of Dirty Harry with the social justice of Dorothy Day when looking at Miller's Daredevil. His only competitor in the world of comics is DC's Batman.

Sadly, two major movies starring an effete and cheesy Ben Affleck (Daredevil) and a beautiful Jennifer Garner (Elektra) attempted to put Miller's characterizations on the big screen. They failed and, in their failure, they put the cinematic future of Daredevil in doubt.

With both the massive success of the Marvel universe in cinema and the rise of Netflix, however, Disney (Marvel's parent company) allowed for the creation of the Marvel TV universe—all centered around New York and several ground-based characters (as opposed to the heroes who fight cosmic battles such as Thor and Captain America). These include Daredevil, Jessica Jones, Luke Cage, the Iron Fist, and the Punisher. All of them cross repeatedly into the shows of the others, with the mini-series *The Defenders* explaining their connections to one another. One need not watch them all, however, to enjoy *Daredevil*. The first two seasons are stories in themselves, and season three takes place a few months after the collapse of a massive complex during the series finale of *The Defenders*.

When the third and final season begins, Murdock wakes up to find himself in the care of the priest and the nuns who had raised him. He, however, has lost his faith. He does not so much fail to believe in God as become convinced that God is a god who manipulates us as puppets for His entertainment. Murdock, who knows his Bible and catechism well, sees only the God who allowed the torture of Job. His loss of faith affects all around him—his neighborhood, his friends, his priest, his nuns, his parish, and even his enemies.

Throughout the third season, Murdock's loss of faith demands the sacrifice of a number of his closest allies, all of whom believe in him, to bring him back to redemption. There's even a "murder in the cathedral" moment as one of Daredevil's closet and most trusted allies dies in the name of Murdock's faith. Throughout the show, people confess, they pray, they talk theology, and they attend Mass. None of it—praise the good Lord—is forced. The writers, directors, and actors have made it as believable, as complex, and as appealing as life itself.

At this point, let me throw the gauntlet down. Not only is season three of *Daredevil* the best of the show's three seasons, it is the best thing to appear on any screen since season one of *Stranger Things*, and, before that, Christopher Nolan's Dark Knight trilogy.

There are a number of things that make this series and story so compelling. First, every person involved brings her or his absolute best to the show. There's nothing cheesy about any of this. It's deadly serious, and the result is a real work of art. Second, *Daredevil* as a show never dumbs itself down. It writes for those who care deeply about this world and the next. Third, it allows the art to linger. When a conversation needs ten minutes, the show gives the characters ten minutes. There are few of the one-liners or cute quips that so many shows and movies have come to rely on appealing to the tapioca-brain dead mass of those demanding to be entertained.

There are also few sharp camera cuts. Indeed, the 11-minute fight scene during Matthew Murdock's escape from a prison in episode four of season three is the single finest of its type that this writer has ever witnessed, rivaled only by the failed bank robbery in Michael Mann's *Heat* (1995). Fans will gush over this, and directors will study its 11 minutes for years to come.

Even Murdock's fighting style is fascinating. He has combined the Irish boxing techniques of his father with a variety of Asian and Asiatic martial arts. When he fights, he fights close. Murdock, it turns out, can only be punched and bruised and cut for so long. Whatever his supernatural powers, invulnerability is not among them.

The Catholicism of *Daredevil's* three seasons is not the velvet piety of EWTN. Rather, it is gritty, complex, and heroic. There's nothing that Father Lantom or the nuns do that makes the viewer cringe in embarrassment. This is the genuine Catholicism of the Jesuits entering North America, not the voluptuousness of early 19th-century Vatican Romanitas. Given all that is happening in the Catholic Church at the moment—the corruption, the scandals, the lies, the manipulations, the accusations among much of the clergy and hierarchy—*Daredevil* demonstrates what a real Catholic does in the face of adversity. He fights, he struggles, and he fights some more. When he questions his faith and goes through "the dark night of the soul," his friends intervene and pick him back up.

I would love to rage at Netflix for canceling this spectacular series. Yet as my wonderfully Catholic grandmother would tell me, let's just be glad it ever existed at all. Amen.

Stranger Things, Season 1
I Once Lived in Hawkins, Indiana

For those of us who came of age in the 1980s, there's been no greater rush of nostalgia in recent years than that provided by Netflix's delightful and ever-engaging eight-part series *Stranger Things*. While I love cinema when done properly and I have no problems with popular culture, I'm by no means a TV junkie. But, every once in a while, something utterly profound comes along, even in the wasteland that is TV culture.

In almost every way, *Stranger Things* captures a brief slice of time perfectly, especially for those of us who attended junior high and high school during Reagan's first term in the White House. The show takes place over just a few days, beginning November 6, 1983, in the mythical but all-too-real town of Hawkins, Indiana. It follows the heroic actions of four seventh-grade boys, a mysterious girl who arrives in town, some siblings and their friends and rivals, a divorced mom, and a broken sheriff. There's also an ominous modern building and complex looming over the normally quiet Hoosier town, a Department of Energy complex. Surrounded by barbed wire and armed guards, and adorned with neo-Stalinist architecture, the building stands out dramatically in the landscape of Hawkins, Indiana, much as the dilapidated Bates house overlooks its accompanying motel in 1960's *Psycho*.

Even the season of the show matters, as November 6 is a date situated in the twilight realm between Halloween and Thanksgiving. No longer colorful or attractive, the remaining leaves on the trees merely hang dead, shriveled and brown, awaiting execution from and with the inevitable first snowfall.

Stranger Things artfully meshes elements of the late cold-war-era Midwest Reagan-driven affluence, libertarian paranoia, New Wave music and progressive electronica, mad science and Leviathan, Dungeons and Dragons, John Carpenter movies, John Hughes movies, David Lynch movies, Hitchcock movies, Stephen King novels, and the *X-Files* to create a complete and satisfying work of art.

Phew. Some critics have railed against the show for stealing the work of others, and it would be impossible to deny this, yet it's also what makes the show so brilliant in so many ways. Exactly because it relies on so much nerd culture of the early 1980s, *Stranger Things* is as once as comfortable as it is unsettling.

The key to the entire epic, though, is its reliance on the essential nerd game of the early 1980s, Dungeons and Dragons (DnD). The five junior-high protagonists are best friends, and they begin and end the eight episodes while playing a DnD campaign. From the moment we first see the boys, they are held in rapt attention by the leader of their specific campaign, the Dungeon Master—the author and referee of their game. As they begin, the most menacing of DnD monsters, a prince of the Demons, a Demogorgon, has arrived. As soon as it appears with its menacing two heads, the players fall into a panic, with one player, Will, sacrificing himself for the group, attacking the Demogorgon rather than protecting himself. His effort fails, though, as he's only rolled a seven out of 20, not enough to destroy the newly emergent beast. The mother calls for supper, adding additional chaos to the enclosed world of fabulism, and the game must end, despite no satisfying conclusion for the boys.

As Will rides his bike home in the dark—something we always did in 1983—the real Demogorgon, having been unleashed by the machinations of the Department of Energy, emerges in a part of town the boys refer to as Mirkwood and takes Will captive, carrying him off to his underground lair.

Reality becomes Dungeons and Dragons, and Dungeons and Dragons becomes reality, at the very beginning of *Stranger Things*. The series opens with an accident—or so it seems—at the Department of Energy complex. Whether the government has unleashed a being from another dimension or the government complex had been intentionally placed on top of a portal to another dimension remains unclear throughout the story. Instead, the viewer only knows that two things emerge at the same time: an eleven-year-old girl named Eleven (presumably after the famous scene involving "going to eleven" in *Spinal Tap*) and the faceless monster that does nothing but kidnap and devour. Whether these two beings represent the two heads of the Demogorgon or they are merely the examples of good and evil also remains unclear throughout the series. What is clear is that the little girl was a normal human girl abducted by the government and raised by the head bureaucrat—named "Papa"—while being experimented upon repeatedly. Now endowed with incredible powers of telekinesis, she behaves as one would expect an abused child to behave: she is at once stunningly brilliant but also seriously damaged.

Again, though, what allows all of this to work—from the government to the monster, to the small town—is the bookending game of Dungeons and Dragons.

Created in the late 1960s and early 1970s by a number of wargamers, but especially by the Wisconsin genius Gary Gygax (1938–2008), DnD became the game of choice for all outsider, geek, and nerd kids (especially boys) in the late 1970s and early 1980s. The jocks wouldn't play it, of course, and neither would the druggies. The former were too busy looking good, and the latter too busy being spaced out. Instead, DnD was the exclusive game of all the "gifted" kids, those deemed hideously uncool by the majority of their peers; the kids who watched *Battlestar Galactica* and *Doctor Who* and who read J. R. R. Tolkien and Terry Brooks without apology and who wrote their seventh-grade theme papers on the effects of atomic warfare on Nagasaki, a space colony on Mars, and the dangers of acid rain. These were the same kids who went to Rush concerts (with the stoners!, if their parents would let them) and who thought *Alien*, *The Thing*, and *Blade Runner* the greatest movies in the history of cinema. They probably read *Starlog* and collected comics as well.

Though the story of Gygax is, ultimately, a rather depressing one, he did manage for a while to combine, successfully, the excitement of fantasy (especially the American pulp and horror works of Robert E. Howard, H. P. Lovecraft, August Derleth, and Fritz Leiber) with the intensity of war gaming, creating an all-too-brief gaming empire, TSR, out of Lake Geneva, Wisconsin.

As mentioned above, this show beautifully blends much of the past to make a very artful present. Without going into details that would give away too many plot elements, the story's themes deal with a natural and healthy fear of government, the omnipresent tapioca conformity of the American middle-class, the need for heroism at all times (no matter the cost of sacrifice), the little things that make community work, and the brokenness of each individual person. While the story has elements of humor, it is a dark and unhappy story without a fulfilling resolution. It is also rather PG-13 at times, involving not just some of the creepiest situations imaginable, but also some not necessarily historically inaccurate sexuality among Midwestern teenagers.

From the opening minute to the closing, nostalgia covered me in waves as I watched all eight episodes. I find it hard if not impossible to look back to the early 1980s and not see the glorious days of friendship and innocence, Dungeons and Dragons, and an almost complete absence of cynicism.

While I only visit now when time and work permit, I once had the grand privilege of living in Hawkins, Indiana. *Stranger Things* has allowed me to remember the fine citizenship I once possessed in that gloriously broken and imaginative community.

Stranger Things, Season 2
Mind Flaying

If there is something better that has been made for the screen (large or small) than *Stranger Things*—at least since the final movie of Christopher Nolan's Dark Knight trilogy came out in 2012—I have certainly missed it. And yet, it's not as if *Stranger Things* is second best in some weird contest of mediocrity. It is, from start to finish, extraordinary. It's extraordinary in its imagination, in its plot, in its making the unreal real, in its embrace of nostalgia, but, most of all, in its full acceptance of the human condition—at once mysterious and full of awe, comprised of beautiful individuals, each deeply flawed. While *Stranger Things* Season 2 is at once better and weaker than Season 1 in its constituent parts, it remains a thing of glory and beauty.

When thinking about the excellence of the show, one might very well wonder, just who are the Duffer Brothers, and where on God's green earth did they come from? Twin-brother creators, writers, and directors, they brought *Stranger Things* to life. Crazily, they did not even enter this whirligig of existence until after Season 1 took place. They were in utero! Somehow, though, they absorbed the culture and deeper meaning of the decade, grasping the nuances of the early Reagan Era—full of tax cuts, unmatched economic growth, acid rain, middle-class pride, the death of Spock, *The Thing*, *Blade Runner*, *Sixteen Candles*, Rush, Yes, Tears for Fears, Echo and the Bunnymen, the imminent if unseen collapse of the Soviet empire, entrepreneurial genius, California ascendancy, Commodore 64s and Macintosh 128s, John Paul II, Stephen King, Steve Jobs, Milton Friedman, and, of course, that greatest of all nerddom games, Advanced Dungeons and Dragons.

Just as important, the Duffer Brothers could only have emerged at the moment that the internet had almost fully decentralized the music and the television industries. Try as they might, the Duffer Brothers found little success with the mainstream channels. In their unrelenting drive for success—never tempered by any desire to compromise their art—they turned to Netflix. Netflix, thank the good Lord, took a chance with the Duffers. The rest, of course, is history. A match made in eternity, but manifested in time.

I am exactly the same age as the female protagonist of *Stranger Things*, Nancy, and Season 1 re-immersed me in my life at Hutchinson High School in ways I never could have expected. Yes, I listened to the pensive early New Order, I played *Dungeons and Dragons*, I loved Reagan, Jobs, and Friedman, and I never stopped reading science fiction or Batman comic books. As with the younger male protagonists of *Stranger Things*, I had but a few very close friends, and my mom let me ride my bike—free-range parenting in those days—from one side of Hutchinson, Kansas, to the other, from dawn to dusk. As long as I was home by dinnertime, no inquiries about my day were made. Was I mischievous? Oh yes. Did I head to the library as often as I caused trouble? Equally, yes. I might very well have been the local king of troublemaking nerds, amazed, to this day, that I didn't kill myself or cause more property damage than I actually did.

While Season 1 of *Stranger Things* brilliantly introduced us to the wildly imaginative and yet comfortably familiar bright and dark worlds of that decaying autumn of 1983, with the government's unleashing of hell upon an unsuspecting Indiana town the day after Guy Fawkes Day, Season 2 begins on October 28, 1984, a little less than a year later. Critically, the second season begins on the eve of the 1984 presidential election, the election that solidified the Reagan Revolution, clearing out the political control of technology, industry, and community and positioning the free world to destroy the tyrannical one. Reagan/Bush signs appear prominently throughout the first several episodes, offering surety and hope.

In Season 1, the heroes were outcast kids, confused teenagers, and broken adults. The enemies were societal conformity, peer pressure, and the U. S. government, especially the Department of Energy. For Season 2, the Duffer Brothers brought the heroes together, still separated by age, but much more aligned in purpose. The new government bureaucrats are not quite heroes, but—lead by Paul Reiser—they are on the side of right. Reaganism has replaced Johnson-Nixon-Carter-era corruption, if not the incompetence.

Though the Duffer Brothers might have taken the easy route with the new season, offering us all-new adventures into their *X-Files*-like Hoosier funhouse of horrors, the twin brothers wisely tackle the far more difficult issues of post-traumatic stress syndrome. The show is never merely about monsters, it's about nightmares, all too real and all too cumbersome for the human condition. In the first season, the adults suffer from their pasts—especially Police Chief Hopper, having served in Vietnam and endured the taunts of the New Left, lost children, and seen his marriage destroyed, now surviving only by crusading against injustice and popping anti-anxiety medication. In this season, we see Will, the boy abducted by the monster, experiencing not only depression but also possession, and the girl, Eleven (Jane), wondering if her new father is holding her back as oppressively as the government once had engineered her. Depressed and confused, neither can find happiness, though each is surrounded by love. These two must enter into the unknown on their own, only coming to realize, penultimately, just how vital they are, not just as individuals, but as friends.

Indeed, if there is one thing that ties together the best of what's humane in the second season of *Stranger Things*, it is the necessity of friendship and community to overcome adversity, no matter how demonic or depraved or bureaucratic. At one critical moment, as a new student named Max, arriving from California with her abusive older brother, asks Michael why he opposes her entrance into their group's intimate friendship, he loses his temper.

Taken as a whole, Season 2 is every bit as great as Season 1. Yet, despite its many successes, its weaknesses make it slightly uneven and even a bit troubling. In the first season, we were treated to something done exceedingly well that is usually done very poorly in the various dramatic arts of the last hundred years. Very few artists can capably create good characters who actually strive to be good and still remain interesting. Most artists—especially in fiction, movies, and television—pander to the easy, bad decisions or they make the good characters one-dimensional and cheesy, usually armed not just with powerful weapons but with cringe-worthy one-liners.

Season 1 of *Stranger Things* introduced deeply flawed heroes, but those heroes struggled mightily against their flaws, always hoping to do what was right, even when hindered by their individual sins, flaws, and failings. As such, even the most troubled of the heroes earned our profound love by remaining, at some fundamental level, innocent. Of course, there was no better character for the viewer than Eleven, the little girl stolen by the U.S. government from her parents, tattooed in the manner of the Jews in the Holocaust, and used brutally as an experiment to further national interests. She killed when necessary, but she strove to find her humanity, despite never having had a good example in her life. We cheered and cheered for Eleven to succeed because she wanted to succeed, but only by doing the right thing and by wanting to love and be loved. Season 1 ended, correctly, with Eleven seemingly sacrificing herself for her friends, the first persons who had ever treated her with respect.

In Season 2, Eleven is understandably angry at the way she's been raised, and she now wants, again understandably, to be with those she loves and to find out why she was abandoned by (stolen from) her parents. Her quest, though, goes all wrong, as she becomes involved with a bombastic, nasty gang of the scuzziest people imaginable. Though she walks away from this gang, she has changed, becoming sleek and cool, rather than innocent and loving. Frankly, I hated to see this change in her, and it made me less sympathetic to the second season. The same thing happens, though, with far less screen time, to Mike's mother, who has gone from a powerfully concerned mom to a bored, sex-craved kitten. It's neither funny nor helpful to the story.

These, however, are minor points in the big scheme of things, and, whatever its faults, Season 2 is still the best thing on any screen at the time of this writing. Those characters we loved in Season 1 are every bit as interesting in the second season, if not more so. Joyce is still the best mom in the world, Hopper is still the best cop in the world, the four boys are the best nerds in the world, and even Steve, so sleazy in Season 1, has become the "good guy," a true leader in the best sense of the word.

And for those of us who actually grew up in the early 1980s, we get to enjoy all the nostalgia, yet again, of the decade that so shaped us.

The demogorgons, the mind flayers, the new wave music, the arcades, the free-range parenting, and the best president of the twentieth century, which so shaped our childhood, are now manifest for all to see and enjoy.

Ave, the Duffer Brothers! Yes, Ave. Pure and simple, Ave.

Stranger Things, Season 4
Friendship in Every Manifestation

Whether extremely good (Season 1) or relatively weak (Season 3), all four seasons of *Stranger Things* have served as a love letter to the 1980s, the decade of *Blade Runner*, Ronald Reagan, shopping malls, Satanic panics, and, to be sure, Kate Bush and Metallica. The nostalgia gloriously permeates every aspect of the show. Indeed, so much of it speaks directly to this 50-something that parts of the show simply make my soul ache in memory. I was in seventh grade when Reagan became president, and I was a senior in college when the Berlin Wall came down. The 1980s, simply put, were my decade, and I deeply appreciate the trouble the Duffer Brothers have taken to recreate that glorious era. I also grew up in a town (though in Kansas) just a little bigger than the fictional Hawkins, IN. I was exactly the same age as Nancy Wheeler; I played lots of Dungeons & Dragons; and Bush's *Hounds of Love* was in constant rotation on my stereo system, especially during my senior year of high school. Admittedly, I wasn't into heavy metal, but I did appreciate it, preferring all things college rock and progressive rock, and I never took, smoked, or partook in any form of illicit or illegal drugs. After all, Nancy Reagan had told us to "just say no." Seemed wise to me. Being raised on Tolkien and Bradbury, I read all the Stephen King I could, and horror was to me the third-finest genre of literature, immediately situated after fantasy and science fiction. I'm only sad that none of the kids in Hawkins seem to have found debate and forensics as a way of life. Then, my nostalgic past would be complete in the Duffers' fictional universe.

As good and as epic as the series ever gets, Season 4 mostly takes place—with several jaunts into the past as well as into the near and immediate future—over a spring-break week, March 1986. As just mentioned, even with its admittedly few flaws, the season is absolutely epic. From the emergence of Lady Applejack to the unleashing of the Upside Down, to the run Max Mayfield takes across a demonic landscape, to Eddie Munson's guitar solo that calls forth a storm of bats, to an escape from a Russian gulag, Season 4 is, without a doubt, wonderfully and intensely over the top.

As with all of *Stranger Things*, Season 4 deals with serious themes, while never losing the humorous elements that make up life. Earlier seasons explored the nature of conspiracy and possession, the nature of ideology and rights, and the struggle of good versus evil, but Season 4 goes to the very source of such things, trying to find a commonality to it all. After all, one might properly ask, why is Hawkins, IN, the center of so much turmoil and horror? In particular, Season 4 grapples with the nature of friendship and community, the dread results of conformity, the progressive inanities of governments (here and abroad), and the essence of heroism and sacrifice. Granted, many of these themes are common to all forms of drama and art, but *Stranger Things* successfully asks these questions again, in a way that speaks truthfully to its audience.

It's worth looking at these four themes in a bit of detail. First, when Season 4 begins, all the main characters of the previous seasons are separated but desperately trying to maintain their friendships and relationships. Lucas and Erica Sinclair, Max, Dustin Henderson, Steve Harrington, Robin Buckley, and Nancy and Mike Wheeler are in Hawkins, and Jane (Eleven), Will, Jonathan, and Joyce Byers are in California. Murray Bauman is in Indianapolis, and, we quickly find out, Jim Hopper is alive and being held and tortured in a Soviet gulag in western Siberia. The essence of Season 4 might very well be the need for these groupings and friendships to come back together. Truly, *Stranger Things* is about friendship in all of its manifestations.

Second, and deeply related to the first point, friendship can thwart tyranny as well as change the direction of the world. Friendship—animated by love—moves the very wheels of the world. We find this especially in Season 4 with Steve and Nancy (and Jonathan), with Mike and Eleven, with Joyce and Hopper, and with Max and Lucas. Without friendship, bullies (whether they're at the level of your local demagogue and your high-school clique or at the level of a nation-state) win. At one point in the first episode, newcomer Eddie Munson, a D&D Dungeon Master and metalhead, decries conformity as the "true monster." In *Stranger Things*, friendship leavens and allows us to become fully ourselves rather than conforming to some inane standard.

Third, *Stranger Things* has always been critical about the nature of government. Season 1, especially, revealed the horrors of scientific progressivism as Dr. Brenner unleashed hell upon Hawkins and upon its children. In Season 4, we see Brenner's backstory and his detailed and gross manipulation of children. He sees them not for what they are (as fully human), but as experiments, to be used and discarded in utilitarian fashion. He "loves" the children, but in a perverted and abusive fashion. Without spoiling the season, it's worth noting that our own American government is deeply divided in the show, but, even in its divisions, it is always utilitarian and self-interested, never seeking the common good or defending the natural rights of the human person.

Additionally, *Stranger Things* shows the true horrors of the Soviet gulag. Not since *The Killing Fields* (1984) had the gulag been shown so brutally on screen. Granted, *Stranger Things* throws some humor and outrageous action sequences into its scenes of the gulag, but it remains the deadly and evil prison camp of Solzhenitsyn's accounts, rivaling anything the Nazis had created.

Finally, fourth, especially through the characters of Steve, Max, and Eddie, *Stranger Things* Season 4 explores the nature of true heroism and its necessary connection to sacrifice. I'll keep this chapter spoiler-free, but let me state that these three characters, especially, reveal the best of human nature and do so in a romantic but also realistic fashion.

None of this, however, should suggest that Season 4 is without its flaws. In ways not always so subtle (especially in contrast with the show as a whole, which can deal with sublime themes very artfully, as just noted), Season 4 awkwardly places questions of sexuality and identity before its audience. These moments come across as forced and seem rather jarring, taking the watcher away from the full immersion the show demands. Additionally, the character of Jonathan—so powerful in Seasons 1 and 2 as the steady big brother—is essentially wasted in Season 4, as he's become, for all intents and purposes, a rather boring stoner. Yet these really are minor quibbles. Most of *Stranger Things* is excellent, and there's no reason to allow these flaws to overshadow the overall greatness of the show.

With Season 4, the Duffer Brothers have proven, yet again, how a series can tell a story so differently than can a single movie. That is, they have figured out exactly how to make art out of the relatively new medium of streaming. Their efforts successfully reveal so many possibilities in the world of cinema. I'm already very much looking forward to returning, yet again, to Hawkins.

Steven Wilson's *Hand. Cannot. Erase.*
An Incarnational Whole

One of the greatest things in this whirligig of a world—however fraught with a string of perilous and gut-wrenching disasters—is the mystery of the human person. And, until God decides to end this existence, every person is a new reflection of the Infinite. From the Catholic Humanist perspective, every human is an unrepeatable center of dignity and freedom. Each person, born in a particular place and time, comes only once, a life to burn brightly or not, for oneself or for another, in the time allotted to each of us. "Dark and inscrutable are the ways in which we come into the world," the grand Anglo-Irish statesman and philosopher Edmund Burke understood. Fewer truths have ever been spoken in such perfect formation of the English language.

Yet, speaking on the mystery of the person and personhood, Pope John Paul II put it even more beautifully in the penultimate month of 1996.

> *The mystery of the Incarnation* has given a tremendous impetus to man's thought and artistic genius. Precisely by reflecting on the union of the two natures, human and divine, in the person of the Incarnate Word, Christian thinkers have come to explain the concept of person as the unique and unrepeatable center of freedom and responsibility, whose inalienable dignity must be recognized. This concept of the person has proved to be the cornerstone of any genuinely human civilization.

As someone who has had the privilege of teaching history and writing biography the entirety of his professional career, I hope and pray that John Paul II's words and ideas reach across everything I teach, think, and write. Thus, I am always looking for new ways to understand the dignity of each individual person, however tragically flawed.

In 2015, such a statement and manifestation of dignity arrived in the most unusual of ways: in the form of a rock concept album by the rather devoutly atheistic, seemingly always grumpy, and unbelievably talented English musician Steven Wilson. His album, a 67-minute story about a lost soul, came out on February 27, 2015. In terms of lyrics and music, Wilson's work is extraordinary by the standards of any genre. What should intrigue us most, however, is the subject matter and how Wilson fills it out. The subject matter is the uniqueness of each human person, and he focuses on the life of one lost soul.

Inspiration

In 2011, a number of British companies joined forces to release a documentary about the tragic real-life death of a rather normal person, Joyce Carol Vincent. Entitled *Dreams of a Life*, the film explored the events—many of them speculative and sometimes verging on gossipy—leading up to the discovery of Vincent's body, decomposed over three years on the couch in her apartment. Presumed to have died around the end of 2003, she had left her TV playing and Christmas presents unopened when three people legally broke into the apartment to check on her in 2006.

The story itself captivated the British imagination. Born in 1965, Vincent had been professional, vivacious, and the youngest of five daughters. How she had gone three years dead with no one checking on her—including her landlord, her siblings, and the utility companies—is one of the most intriguing aspects of the story.

Frankly, the film as film is rather weak, even if the story and the subject matter are stunning and terrifying. So many talking heads appear throughout *Dreams of a Life*—most of whom are unidentified and given no context but allowed to speak whatever theory they want—that the tragedy of the loss of Vincent becomes merely a catalyst for lots and lots of people to speculate about what actually happened. Unfortunately, *Dreams of a Life* becomes something of a bad and very long news report, all told by the "man on the street" who, in reality, knows nothing but believes everything.

Ultimately, though, beyond the superficial aspect of the interviews, the film asks how any person could be so utterly lost in our modern, urban society that she goes missing for three years with almost no attention from any family member, neighbor, or even business in the larger society.

Hand. Cannot. Erase.

When musician Steven Wilson saw the film, he, too, became intrigued by the very loss of a human soul, the loss of a life, and the loss of a unique person. In a phone interview with American journalist Stephen Humphries, Wilson explained the role of the film:

> There was something very symbolic about the story of Joyce Carol Vincent: this was a young woman living in the heart of the city who chose to erase herself, to disappear. If you really want to disappear, you wouldn't go to live in a small village in the country, you would go live in the heart of the city. You would go and live in the midst of millions of other people. If you do that, you will disappear.

To be fair, many of Wilson's albums over the past two decades have dealt just with such alienation from society, but they have usually done so by looking at how certain behaviors lead one to become alienated. The story of Joyce Carol Vincent is not so clear-cut. In many ways, it is not just about a person exiling herself from society, but also about a society—by its sins of omission—exiling her as well.

In creating his own 67-minute concept album, Wilson chose to give his character a happier ending than the real-life analogue. Still, the events of Wilson's fictional life are horrific, as anyone who has lost a child knows all too deeply and all too permanently.

In the most powerful track of the album, "Routine," our protagonist deals with the loss of her entire family. Though the words are mundane when taken piece by piece, when taken as a whole, they are sublime.

> What do I do with all the children's clothes?
> Such tiny things that still smell of them
> And the footprints in the hallway
> Onto my knees, scrub them away
> —"Routine"

The life and lost love of her deceased family haunts every aspect of her being. To cope, but to keep moving, to become almost heart- and soul-dead, seems the only sure way to survive the debilitations of loss and survivor's guilt.

Hand. Cannot. Erase. considers a number of moods and emotions tied to loss and the desire of the depressed self to disappear from all around her. About fifty-five minutes into the album, however, memories of love reawaken the protagonist. In particular, it is the love of her ancestors that enlivens her again, filling her with some kind of calling and purpose.

> Come child
> Come back if you want to
> Come back if you want to
> Come back
>
> A bicycle
> A garden wall
> A mother's call
> A love is born
> And after all the sleep that falls on me
> —"Ancestral"

"Ancestral" flows immediately into "Happy Returns," the title revealing the protagonist's happy if somewhat reluctant and reticent return to real life. "Hey brother, I feel like I'm living in parentheses." Whatever regrets she might have had, however, the listener knows the lead character made it back from her depression and her own exile. Unlike the real-life story of Joyce Carol Vincent, Wilson's hero re-emerges from the shades, broken but ready to find some healing, however slight it might be, yet preferable to eternal darkness and the annihilation of the self in the abyss.

Art, but Then Some

Taking his own excellent and expertly treated art to the next level, Wilson also released a book to accompany the album. Roughly the same dimensions as a vinyl LP, but as thick as a coffee-table book, the book *Hand. Cannot. Erase.* details the life of his protagonist in ways his music simply cannot. Beautifully illustrated throughout, the book gives the reader something unique: various media that allow us to fall into the world of the heroine. Not only do we experience her world through photography, but we also get to look at her birth certificate; her diary; the sleeve notes of a mixtape; a postcard;

newspaper clippings; sketchings; and, most importantly, a note to her brother, declaring her re-emergence in the world. These are not simply parts of the book, but removable and tangible media.

When I was a child, I used to spend hours looking at the gatefold sleeves of Yes's live triple album, *Yessongs*. Not only did I love the music, but I cherished and obsessed over the fantasy paintings by Roger Dean. Floating islands, organic star ships, and alien fish came together in a rather forceful and fantastic way.

With the release of *Hand. Cannot. Erase.*—the title strongly hinting at the ultimate optimism of the story—Wilson has taken the release of an album to an entirely new level. Not only can we enjoy the music, aurally, but Wilson has given us a life to study with our ears, our eyes, and our hands. Even more importantly, we can connect to the life of his fictional character at the level of the mind, the heart, and the soul.

Whatever else it did, good or bad, the Protestant Reformation separated the image from the word at a most fundamental and almost irredeemable level. Over the last 500 years, western culture has striven mightily to bring the two back together in an incarnational fashion. When image and word become one, as John Paul II said in 1996, we can rediscover the refashioning of the human person, broken but destined for sanctity.

Perhaps one of the greatest and most telling ironies of the modern world is that a self-professed English atheist has rediscovered one of the most beautiful manifestations of human dignity yet conceived. Through music, image, and word, we find a lost person, a person alienated from society by her own actions as well as by those taken by other members of society. Unlike the real and tragic Joyce Carol Vincent, Steven Wilson's heroine experiences love and loss, but, as she drowns in her own wallowing depression, she comes up for air and finds meaning again—slowly—through her relations, ancestral and current.

If this isn't the essence of a Catholic Humanism, nothing is.

Here in Wilson's high art, we find the absolute best of humanism. Now, we just need to remind those who love humanism that it is only properly understood and completed when it is modified by that all-important word: Catholic.

What If?
The Moral Imagination of Disney's
Beauty and the Beast

One night, I very reluctantly watched Disney's 2017 live version of *Beauty and the Beast*. I must admit three things before I get into the heart of this chapter. First, I've never been anti-Disney. I know many conservatives think Disney is the end of civilization, but I've never seen it that way. Like comic-book superheroes, Disney, at its best, has served to teach us and remind us of long-forgotten myths, fables, parables, and old wives' tales. And I would never hesitate to put a movie such as *Sleeping Beauty* among my top ten or fifteen movies of all time. I even enjoyed the original animated *Beauty and the Beast* when it came out over twenty years ago, though I didn't love it.

Second, I have, from as far back as I can remember, despised musicals. *The Sound of Music* is tolerable, but nothing else! I'm sure this is some deficiency on my part, but it remains a very strong prejudice, right or wrong.

Third, I agreed to watch the *Beauty and the Beast* ONLY to try to be a good father to my daughters. They adored the movie in theaters and could barely contain themselves when I bought them the Blu-ray version.

As I started watching the movie with my daughters, I was distracted, checking out some things on my iPad and barely paying attention. Oh look, there's Hermione. Oh look, there's Kevin Kline. Oh look, that set of a French village is nice. About ten minutes into the movie, however, I was completely hooked. I put the iPad down, and I was fully a part of the movie from ten minutes in until its end. Had I been paying a bit more attention in the first several minutes, I would have seen some significant and critical clues to the meaning of the film. I allowed (through my own free will, admittedly) the devices of post-modernity to distract me. Ugh.

You probably already know the story. A beautiful young woman named, appropriately enough, Belle, finds the life of her French village too provincial. She wants to read and learn and travel and explore. Her father is a kind of wacky mad inventor of the late-18th-century Ben-Franklin variety, and their neighbors think them truly odd. The local bully, Gaston, is a war hero, and, strangely, beloved by the community. Because he's the most arrogant, he thinks he should marry Belle, she being the most beautiful. Somewhere outside of town, a local prince has so angered an enchantress—because he lacks charity—that she turns him into a demonic Beast and entraps his servants as utensils (tools). A crown of thorns grows over the castle, and it is perpetually shrouded by fog and ice, trapped in its own lack of grace. Even the locals have their memory erased that such a manor or castle ever existed to protect their village. The enchantress gives the Beast a rose. When the last pedal has fallen—should he not find true love—he and his servants remain permanently disfigured. When the father is captured by the Beast as a prisoner, Belle takes his place. Soon, Belle realizes the goodness that is at the heart of the Beast and falls in love with him. In the meantime, the father convinces the village that the Beast is real (the plot is a bit more complicated, but not too much). Gaston leads an uprising against the Beast, but is defeated. With his defeat, the enchantress returns, lifting the spell from the Beast, and he becomes the true prince again. All of his servants reclaim their human form, and the villagers remember the prince and the castle. Accordingly, they offer their allegiance to the reborn prince and his now wife, Belle.

Phew. Now, that's a fairy story!

If you'll indulge me, let me quote at great length a passage most of you have read before, Edmund Burke's famous writing about the moral imagination.

> But now all is to be changed. All the pleasing illusions, which made power gentle, and obedience liberal, which harmonized the different shades of life, and which, by a bland assimilation, incorporated into politics the sentiments which beautify and soften private society, are to be dissolved by this new conquering empire of light and reason. All the decent drapery of life is to be rudely torn off. All the superadded ideas, furnished from the wardrobe of a moral imagination, which the heart owns, and the understanding

ratifies, as necessary to cover the defects of our naked shivering nature, and to raise it to dignity in our own estimation, are to be exploded as a ridiculous, absurd, and antiquated fashion. On this scheme of things, a king is but a man; a queen is but a woman; a woman is but an animal; and an animal not of the highest order. All homage paid to the sex in general as such, and without distinct views, is to be regarded as romance and folly. Regicide, and parricide, and sacrilege, are but fictions of superstition, corrupting jurisprudence by destroying its simplicity. The murder of a king, or a queen, or a bishop, or a father, are only common homicide; and if the people are by any chance, or in any way gainers by it, a sort of homicide much the most pardonable, and into which we ought not to make too severe a scrutiny. On the scheme of this barbarous philosophy, which is the offspring of cold hearts and muddy understandings, and which is as void of solid wisdom, as it is destitute of all taste and elegance, laws are to be supported only by their own terrors, and by the concern which each individual may find in them from his own private speculations, or can spare to them from his own private interests.

As I watched the live version of *Beauty and the Beast*, I found myself utterly taken with the movie—emotionally as well as intellectually—and I slowly realized why. The story is the oldest story in the Christian world. It's the story about love, sacrifice, and redemption. The beast is a beast because of his poor choices. When he encounters real love and sacrifice, he understands his own folly and, most importantly, learns to sacrifice himself for others. He is, symbolically and literally, reborn. The Redeemer removes his skin and baptizes him in the blood of the Lamb. The enchantress might be a bit pagan, but she's equally a bit archangel and the Virgin Mary. Belle, beautiful and bookish, is the personification of Grace itself.

As the movie was ending, I thought, I might very well be reading too much into this, wanting to find Christianity in the story simply because I fell in love with the story. Then, my patience and thought were more than rewarded. As the spell is lifted from the castle of the Beast, the last thing to transform is the very top of the castle, a rather eerie gargoyle overlooking the cursed realm. When it changes, it doesn't just become less creepy, it becomes truly holy. The gargoyle transforms into St. Michael slaying the devil. Truly, literally. Right there on a Hollywood movie screen—seen by millions of moviegoers—is the symbol of the entire movie, a statue of St. Michael in victory against the devil. How amazing is that?

This should leave us with one question. Why quote Burke above? Well, here are two answers that I hope are sufficient. First, Burke, of course, tells us about the moral imagination. What is it but the ability to see the best of a person, the very creative act of God, living within one's soul and within the body, a temple of the Holy Spirit, no matter how much corruption we have placed upon ourselves because of our poor choices? Only Belle's moral imagination allows her to see past the demonic form of the Beast, and only this trust and faith on her part allows the Beast to claim that grace that Christ gave to us all on a Friday afternoon at a place of skulls.

Second, the setting of *Beauty and the Beast* takes place in a mythical France in the late 18th century. Gaston, the arrogant peasant, even claims that he's felt nothing but boredom since the war ended. Presumably, the war was the Great War for Empire, 1756–1763. The story of *Beauty and the Beast* is a story of "what if?" to be sure.

But what is the "what if"?

What if the French Revolutionaries failed? The Beast, having taxed the villagers for his own aggrandizement, has brought upon himself the wrath of God—through the figure of the Enchantress. The story does not end with the peasants overthrowing the prince, but with the prince being re-baptized, the leader of the rebellion (the French Revolutionary Gaston) killed, and the monarchy restored. Made clean, France avoids the Revolution and "lives happily ever after."

Edmund Burke would approve. And so should we.

If you've not seen the movie yet, do yourself a favor—whether you have daughters, granddaughters, or not—and enjoy every moment of the movie. Had I been paying attention at the beginning of the film, I would have noticed a really critical and beautiful thing. At the top of the Disney Castle (at exactly 13 seconds into the film) stands none other than St. Michael, victorious against not just any enemy, but THE Enemy. Thank you, Disney. You have done a good, good thing, and you have done it mightily.

Part IV: The Moral Imagination & Belief

Oh, White Lady: Faith as a Struggle

Faith has always been a struggle for me. Indeed, throughout my fifty-plus years of life, very rarely have I ever felt comfortable for any stretch of time with my religion or my religious practices.

I readily and rather gleefully abandoned almost any faith and religious observance during my teenage years. I'm not totally sure what I embraced as a substitute, but it certainly wasn't any form of orthodoxy. I rather prided myself on "being good" without needing what I considered as a handicap, religion. I also thought that if God existed, he must be one of the most evil beings ever to exist. The stories of the Old Testament—plagues and wars—horrified me, God the Father looking little better than Stalin or Hitler. The story of Abraham and his willingness to sacrifice Isaac sickened me. To the much younger me, Abraham's duty was to call God a tyrant and defy his commands, even if unto Hell itself.

That God the Father allowed his only son to die on the cross made Him even worse in my eyes. I admired Jesus (and still do—even if only a person; though I accept orthodoxy on this issue, if not always easily), but I thought God the Father downright evil. If He gave over His son, wouldn't He give any one of us over to the enemy at any moment?

There was, to my mind, no trusting him. I never liked King David, either. Anyone who would betray his wife and his friend (Uriah) could never be a hero. And, that God forgave him and that Solomon came from his illicit relationship (I've always loved Solomon) confused me even more.

My childhood Catholicism was such a paradox. I saw so many truly good and wholesome and often saintlike persons who were deeply Catholic. But I also saw so much hypocrisy—in and out of my parish. I saw neglect of what was beautiful as well, and I became convinced that all modern Catholicism (and all faith) was a sham, a slowly dying relic, murdered by degrees by its own adherents. At least, murdered by the young adults of that time. So much religious worship and religious study seemed to be little more than kiddie

211

time, dumbed-down sap, precious moments for idiots. I craved real answers to ponder, not platitudes to memorize and parrot.

Outside of Catholicism and Judaism (over which I was rather obsessed throughout my teen years; its rituals and its history, ancient and modern), I thought Protestant Christianity even more a sham. My image of Protestant Christianity was of entrepreneurial, plastic televangelists. The Tammy Fay Bakers of the world seemed rather normal in this non-Catholic scheme of things. They sickened me then, and they still sicken me today. As self-righteous as Bono was—"My God isn't short of cash, Mr."—he was right. What a lot of hypocrites they all seemed to me in my teenage years.

Yet, again—the personal witness of my maternal grandparents, of a great-aunt and a great-uncle, and even of my hero, J. R. R. Tolkien, all caused me to pause and rethink my own childhood (childish?) dislike of Catholicism. These people really did lead holy and loving lives, they really believed in the teachings of the Church (though all were a bit freaked out by post-Vatican II culture and changes).

And, of course, there was also John Paul II. No one in their right mind could dislike him, then or now.

For a variety of reasons—all too much to go into here—I re-found my faith in Christianity (Catholicism) in the deserts of North Africa in February 1988, and after innumerable talks with my cease-lessly patient roommate and friend, Kevin McCormick, now a beloved and well-known classical guitarist and composer. A Basque theologian in the spring semester of 1988 (at the University of Innsbruck, Austria) helped immensely as well.

Witnesses

Of those I admired most—that is, the Catholics who bore witness to all of the love and best of Christianity—each had a special devotion to the Holy Eucharist and to Jesus's mother. These two devotions have always impressed me. While I certainly thought and think some Catholics take their love of Mary, the Mother of Jesus, too far and into dangerous territory (but, really, who am I to judge?), I have always found those who didn't love Mary far more perplexing. In my own life, I have flirted with a number of other religions, both east and west. But what held me back from becoming Protestant has

212

always been what seems to be the unreality of ignoring or, at best, neglecting Mary. I'm fairly certain that if and when I ever leave Catholicism, it will be toward the East, not the West. Toward Constantinople, not Geneva.

With Brian Wilson, I can easily sing: "God only knows what I'd be without you." With Paul McCartney, "Mother Mary, comfort me."

Really, who couldn't love Mary, the young woman who so gladly and joyously accepted the message of the archangel, who bore the burden of pregnancy, who raised a God-boy, and who stood with him as the Romans drove nails into his flesh, his entire body dripping with blood and seared with wounds? What parent cannot put him or herself in the place of this mother? Whatever one thinks of the theology of Mary, she was one of the most amazing persons in all of world history.

Additionally, Mary plays such a critical role—if only historically, leaving aside theology for a moment—in the development of post-Christian (meaning, post-Jesus) culture. The love, the admiration, and the respect afforded women has come best from Christianity because of the role Mary has played.

I also firmly believe (again, historically if not always theologically) that no western culture or church can embrace and understand the deepest levels of culture and beauty without Mary. She is the symbol of all that is good, holy, and pure. Not a single one of us will ever be Jesus. We will never be fully God and fully man (leaving aside questions of sanctification and Christification), but we can certainly attain (or come very close to) the status of Mary. Think about her words: "My soul doth magnify the Lord." In other words, Mary states quite clearly, she is not God, but she will do—in full obedience—what God wills for her. Her will becomes God's will. I think I can state, even as a pathetic excuse for a Christian, that no person can attain anything higher in this world.

Theologically, I also believe that Mary is the woman of the Apocalypse (Revelation 12), the woman about to be devoured by the dragon. But this belief is incidental to this conclusion.

Everything listed above is true, objectively, at least to my mind, without this last statement of faith.

White Ladies

Being influenced by J. R. R. Tolkien and C. S. Lewis, I'm also not surprised by how often Marian figures appear in history, before and after Mary's actual life on this earth.

In the *Crito*, Socrates reveals that a woman in white appeared to him in a dream, assuring him that in three days he would dwell in the Realm of Pythia. Socrates assures his astounded friend Crito that all would be well.

Venus found her troubled son in a glade. There she handed him weapons of divine making. With them, he remade the Tiber and the West.

Far to the north and a millennium later, the Lady of the Lake approached a young Celt and offered him the sword to unite all peoples in a kingdom dedicated to spring and human flourishing. He accepted.

In the Central Valley of northern New Spain, a pregnant woman in the form of an Aztec goddess appeared to an Indian peasant, asking him to pray for, advocate for, and protect the innocent. He delivered the message to a skeptical world.

Not long after the storming of the Vatican by armed revolutionaries, a tender French girl found a spring that offered the health of the heavens.

Across the ocean at the same moment rode a black-robed Belgian Jesuit across the northern Great Plains, armed only with his breviary and his high, shimmering flag of the Virgin Mary. To the natives, he proclaimed peace, justice, and love, and they, in turned, admired Father Peter-Jean DeSmet like no other.

They must have thought as well that the woman he so cherished seemed much like the ancient law-giver, the White Buffalo Woman, who once appeared to two Lakota warriors, teaching them how to live honorably and well.

The Mother of God revealed herself to King Alfred the Great, promising him right but not comfort if he chose the path of truth. "Out of the mouth of the Mother of God go I," the once and future king proclaimed. At least, this is what a man named Gilbert claimed.

Oh, White Lady: Faith as a Struggle

On the eve of Lenin's victory against the third Rome, a beautiful woman descended from the sky and told three Iberian children of a devastation that would come upon the earth for a century. Those who doubted and those who believed witnessed the falling of the sun. Thousands proclaimed it.

"Lady, three white leopards sat under a juniper tree in the cool of the day." This day was Ash Wednesday. "She honors the Virgin in meditation; we shine in brightness." Old Tom saw it all.

Somewhere in a hell on earth, a small farmer who possessed no confidence, but an overabundance of loyalty, found himself in prayer to Elbereth, Queen of the Heavens. He prayed in a language he did not know and was given the vision of a white star, which he beheld with all of the hope that has ever existed on this side of eternity. Well, so an Oxford don reported.

An image of Jesus's Mom turned a pope's head and torso, preventing an assassin's bullet—by a mere millimeter—from killing the greatest of 20th-century Polish knights. You do know that the Poles exist to remind the rest of us of what can be endured in this world of sorrow. It was a fateful season, the spring of 1981, when a man named Karol barely lived.

Only a few days later, the fortieth president of the United States opened his war of rhetoric against Soviet communism in South Bend, Indiana, under a golden dome and under a golden statue, indeed, under the patronage of Our Lady of the Lakes, Notre Dame du Lac. I was there, and I can confirm what I write.

This man, too, had faced an assassin. He soon laughed about it, but he offered pity and forgiveness for the one who harmed him. As an Armenian nun later told him, he simply had too much to accomplish to fall victim to such evils. Eight short years later, he won. So did we all. Whoever said Excalibur is a myth? What a fool.

Visions Abound: We Only Have to Open Our Eyes. And souls.

Of course, I've never seen a white woman descend from the sky or the sun dance. The Mother of my Lord has never appeared to me and offered me a helmet of piety or a sword of unity, of divine or mundane origins. She's never given me visions of demons or ideology ravaging the face of the earth.

But I have seen Mary many times, and, most likely, you have as well. I have seen her in the embrace of my grandmother. I have seen her in the wisdom of my wife. And I have seen her in the love of my daughters.

A broken stone, inscribed with runic sagacity, sits upon a little rose. That little rose bears a profound name: Cecilia. She spends her days and nights honoring the Lady. She does so through song, dance, and incessant giggling.

Ave

In proper theology, Catholics believe that Mary always points—and must always point—to her son.

I'm not here to prove or disprove this, to affirm or to deny. But, as a historian, as a grandson, as a husband, and as a father, I can state the following without hesitation or trepidation. Our Lady is the symbol of everything that pure, true, good, and beautiful in this world.

Even in my own sinfulness, my ambition, and my doubt, Mary continues to call to me. Come home. Meet my Son.

I'm trying, Mary. I promise.

Oh, Mother Mary, we beg you, "Pray for us now, and at the hour of our death."

Ingram Content Group UK Ltd.
Milton Keynes UK
UKHW042038270423
420913UK00012B/179/J